Social Contracts for Development

AFRICA DEVELOPMENT FORUM

Social Contracts for Development

Bargaining, Contention, and Social Inclusion in Sub-Saharan Africa

Mathieu Cloutier, Bernard Harborne,
Deborah Isser, Indhira Santos,
and Michael Watts

A copublication of the Agence française de développement and the World Bank

Africa Development Forum Series

The **Africa Development Forum Series** was created in 2009 to focus on issues of significant relevance to Sub-Saharan Africa's social and economic development. Its aim is both to record the state of the art on a specific topic and to contribute to ongoing local, regional, and global policy debates. It is designed specifically to provide practitioners, scholars, and students with the most up-to-date research results while highlighting the promise, challenges, and opportunities that exist on the continent.

The series is sponsored by Agence française de développement and the World Bank. The manuscripts chosen for publication represent the highest quality in each institution and have been selected for their relevance to the development agenda. Working together with a shared sense of mission and interdisciplinary purpose, the two institutions are committed to a common search for new insights and new ways of analyzing the development realities of the Sub-Saharan Africa region.

Advisory Committee Members

Agence française de développement
Thomas Mélonio, Executive Director, Research and Knowledge Directorate
Hélène Djoufelkit, Director, Head of Economic Assessment and Public Policy Department
Marie-Pierre Nicollet, Director, Head of Knowledge Department on Sustainable Development
Sophie Chauvin, Head, Edition and Publication Division

World Bank
Albert G. Zeufack, Chief Economist, Africa Region
César Calderón, Lead Economist, Africa Region
Chorching Goh, Lead Economist, Africa Region

Sub-Saharan Africa

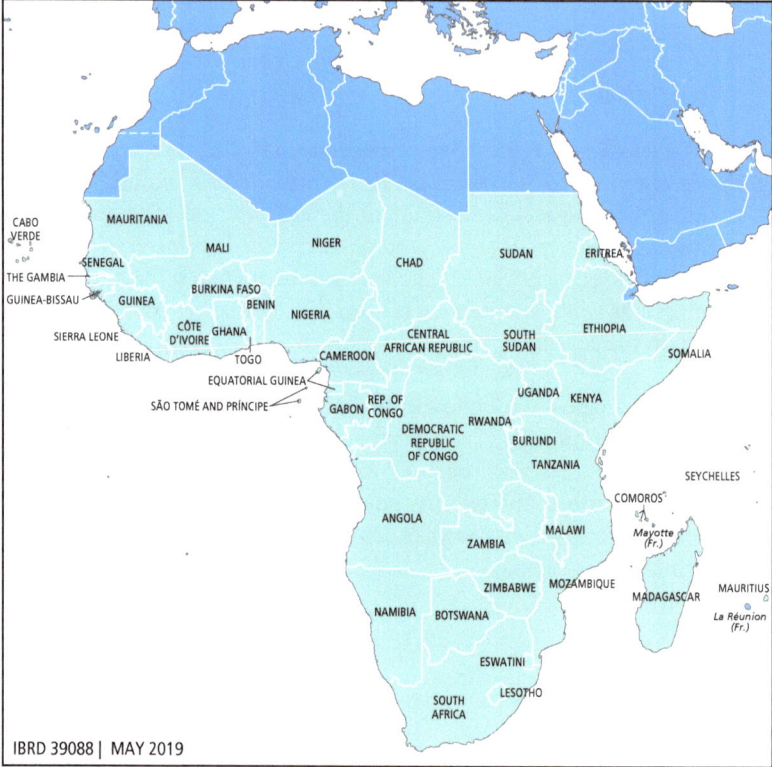

IBRD 39088 | MAY 2019

Source: World Bank (IBRD 39088, May 2019).

Titles in the Africa Development Forum Series

2021

Social Contracts for Development: Bargaining, Contention, and Social Inclusion in Sub-Saharan Africa (2021), Mathieu Cloutier, Bernard Harborne, Deborah Isser, Indhira Santos, Michael Watts

Industrialization in Sub-Saharan Africa: Seizing Opportunities in Global Value Chains (2021), Kaleb G. Abreha, Woubet Kassa, Emmanuel K. K. Lartey, Taye A. Mengistae, Solomon Owusu, Albert G. Zeufack

Food Systems in Africa: Rethinking the Role of Markets (2021), *Les systèmes agroalimentaires en Afrique. Repenser le rôle des marchés* (2020), Gaelle Balineau, Arthur Bauer, Martin Kessler, Nicole Madariaga

2020

The Future of Work in Africa: Harnessing the Potential of Digital Technologies for All (2020), *L'avenir du travail en Afrique : exploiter le potentiel des technologies numériques pour un monde du travail plus inclusif* (2021), Jieun Choi, Mark A. Dutz, Zainab Usman (eds.)

2019

Electricity Access in Sub-Saharan Africa: Uptake, Reliability, and Complementary Factors for Economic Impact (2019), *Accès à l'électricité en Afrique subsaharienne : adoption, fiabilité et facteurs complémentaires d'impact économique* (2020), Moussa P. Blimpo, Malcolm Cosgrove-Davies

The Skills Balancing Act in Sub-Saharan Africa: Investing in Skills for Productivity, Inclusivity, and Adaptability (2019), *Le développement des compétences en Afrique subsaharienne, un exercice d'équilibre : Investir dans les compétences pour la productivité, l'inclusion et l'adaptabilité* (2020), Omar Arias, David K. Evans, Indhira Santos

All Hands on Deck: Reducing Stunting through Multisectoral Efforts in Sub-Saharan Africa (2019), Emmanuel Skoufias, Katja Vinha, Ryoko Sato

2018

Realizing the Full Potential of Social Safety Nets in Africa (2018), Kathleen Beegle, Aline Coudouel, Emma Monsalve (eds.)

Facing Forward: Schooling for Learning in Africa (2018), *Perspectives : l'école au service de l'apprentissage en Afrique* (2019), Sajitha Bashir, Marlaine Lockheed, Elizabeth Ninan, Jee-Peng Tan

2017

Reaping Richer Returns: Public Spending Priorities for African Agriculture Productivity Growth (2017), Obtenir de meilleurs résultats : priorités en matière de dépenses publiques pour les gains de productivité de l'agriculture africaine (2020), Aparajita Goyal, John Nash

Mining in Africa: Are Local Communities Better Off? (2017), L'exploitation minière en Afrique : les communautés locales en tirent-elles parti? (2020), Punam Chuhan-Pole, Andrew L. Dabalen, Bryan Christopher Land

2016

Confronting Drought in Africa's Drylands: Opportunities for Enhancing Resilience (2016), Raffaello Cervigni, Michael Morris (eds.)

2015

Safety Nets in Africa: Effective Mechanisms to Reach the Poor and Most Vulnerable (2015), Les filets sociaux en Afrique : méthodes efficaces pour cibler les populations pauvres et vulnérables en Afrique subsaharienne (2015), Carlo del Ninno, Bradford Mills (eds.)

Land Delivery Systems in West African Cities: The Example of Bamako, Mali (2015), Le système d'approvisionnement en terres dans les villes d'Afrique de l'Ouest : l'exemple de Bamako (2015), Alain Durand-Lasserve, Maÿlis Durand-Lasserve, Harris Selod

Enhancing the Climate Resilience of Africa's Infrastructure: The Power and Water Sectors (2015), Raffaello Cervigni, Rikard Liden, James E. Neumann, Kenneth M. Strzepek (eds.)

Africa's Demographic Transition: Dividend or Disaster? (2015), La transition démographique de l'Afrique : dividende ou catastrophe ? (2016), David Canning, Sangeeta Raja, Abdo Yazbech

Challenge of Fragility and Security in West Africa (2015), Alexandre Marc, Neelam Verjee, Stephen Mogaka

Highways to Success or Byways to Waste: Estimating the Economic Benefits of Roads in Africa (2015), Ali A. Rubaba, Federico Barra, Claudia Berg, Richard Damania, John Nash, Jason Russ

2014

Youth Employment in Sub-Saharan Africa (2014), L'emploi des jeunes en Afrique subsaharienne (2014), Deon Filmer, Louise Fox

Tourism in Africa: Harnessing Tourism for Growth and Improved Livelihoods (2014), Iain Christie, Eneida Fernandes, Hannah Messerli, Louise Twining-Ward

2013

The Political Economy of Decentralization in Sub-Saharan Africa: A New Implementation Model (2013), Bernard Dafflon, Thierry Madiès (eds.)

Empowering Women: Legal Rights and Economic Opportunities in Africa (2013), Mary Hallward-Driemeier, Tazeen Hasan

Les marchés urbains du travail en Afrique subsaharienne (2013), *Urban Labor Markets in Sub-Saharan Africa* (2013), Philippe De Vreyer, François Roubaud (eds.)

Securing Africa's Land for Shared Prosperity: A Program to Scale Up Reforms and Investments (2013), Frank F. K. Byamugisha

2012

Light Manufacturing in Africa: Targeted Policies to Enhance Private Investment and Create Jobs (2012), *L'Industrie légère en Afrique : politiques ciblées pour susciter l'investissement privé et créer des emplois* (2012), Hinh T. Dinh, Vincent Palmade, Vandana Chandra, Frances Cossar

Informal Sector in Francophone Africa: Firm Size, Productivity, and Institutions (2012), *Les entreprises informelles de l'Afrique de l'ouest francophone : taille, productivité et institutions* (2012), Nancy Benjamin, Ahmadou Aly Mbaye

Financing Africa's Cities: The Imperative of Local Investment (2012), *Financer les villes d'Afrique : l'enjeu de l'investissement local* (2012), Thierry Paulais

Structural Transformation and Rural Change Revisited: Challenges for Late Developing Countries in a Globalizing World (2012), *Transformations rurales et développement : les défis du changement structurel dans un monde globalisé* (2013), Bruno Losch, Sandrine Fréguin-Gresh, Eric Thomas White

2011

Contemporary Migration to South Africa: A Regional Development Issue (2011), Aurelia Segatti, Loren Landau (eds.)

L'Économie politique de la décentralisation dans quatre pays d'Afrique subsaharienne : Burkina Faso, Sénégal, Ghana et Kenya (2011), Bernard Dafflon, Thierry Madiès (eds.)

2010

Africa's Infrastructure: A Time for Transformation (2010), *Infrastructures africaines, une transformation impérative* (2010), Vivien Foster, Cecilia Briceño-Garmendia (eds.)

Gender Disparities in Africa's Labor Market (2010), Jorge Saba Arbache, Alexandre Kolev, Ewa Filipiak (eds.)

Challenges for African Agriculture (2010), Jean-Claude Deveze (ed.)

All books in the Africa Development Forum series that were copublished by Agence française de développement and the World Bank are available for free at https://openknowledge.worldbank.org/handle/10986/2150.

Contents

Boxes

Figures

Tables

Acknowledgments

This report is an outcome of a three-year collaboration between World Bank Global Practices including Social Protection and Jobs (SPJ), Governance (GGP), and Social Sustainability and Inclusion (SSI). The work was led by Indhira Santos (senior economist, SPJ), Deborah Isser (lead governance specialist, GGP), and Bernard Harborne (lead technical specialist, SSI), with Mathieu Cloutier (economist, GGP). The work was initially led by Iamele Rigolini (lead economist, SPJ). The team benefited from two key advisers: Michael Watts, professor emeritus, University of California, Berkeley, and Belinda Archibong, associate professor, Barnard College.

This work was commissioned by and was conducted under the overall guidance of the chief economist for Africa, Albert Zeufack, with support from Robert S. Chase (practice manager, SPJ) and Dena Ringold (director, Human Development).

Many academics and researchers were involved in the work, including Aisha Ahmad, associate professor, University of Toronto; Kristina Bentley, senior researcher, University of Cape Town; Mamadou Diouf, professor, Columbia University; James Habyarimana, associate professor, Georgetown University; Tim Kelsall, senior research fellow, Overseas Development Institute; Maty Konte, associate professor, University of Maastricht; Peter Lewis, professor, Johns Hopkins University; Erin McCandless, associate professor, University of Witwatersrand; Lisa Mueller, associate professor, Macalester College; Cyril Obi, director of African Peacebuilding, New York; Ada Ordor, associate professor, University of Cape Town; Danielle Resnick, senior research fellow, International Food Policy Research Institute; Abdi Samatar, professor, University of Minnesota; Mahaman Tidjani Alou, professor, Abdou Moumouni University; and Leonard Wantchekon, professor, Princeton University.

The work is part of the Africa regional studies on development and was financed by the Chief Economist's Office. The study also received generous support from the World Bank's Human Rights and Development Trust Fund.

About the Authors

Mathieu Cloutier is an economist in the francophone West Africa unit of the World Bank's Governance Global Practice. His operational and lending supervision work includes decentralization, service delivery, and public finance management projects with a special focus on the Sahel and fragile countries such as Mali and Niger. He has also been involved in knowledge and analytics products centered on political economy, citizen engagement, domestic resources mobilization, and state-owned enterprises. Recently, he led the development of an empirical framework for social contract diagnostics for the regional report, *Social Contract for Stability, Equity and Prosperity in Africa*. The empirical framework is currently being applied in multiple settings for country assessments and Systematic Country Diagnostics. Before joining the World Bank in 2017 as a Young Professional, Mathieu obtained a PhD in economics from the University of Chicago. His doctoral research investigated the impact of decentralization on corruption and bribes paid by firms to local officials.

Bernard Harborne is a lead technical specialist in the Social Sustainability and Inclusion Global Practice of the World Bank. He joined the Bank in 2004 as the lead conflict adviser for Africa, including serving as country manager in Côte d'Ivoire. In various positions, he has led the World Bank's work on conflict assessments, engagement in peace processes (five to date), and the integration of geospatial data into risk analytics. He has authored or coauthored five country engagement strategies, most recently during the crises in the Central African Republic, Libya, and South Sudan. He has managed projects for the demobilization and reintegration of ex-combatants as well as local and community driven–development in conflict-affected countries. He is the lead on the World Bank's security sector work and was the principal author of the sourcebook, *Securing Development: Public Finance and the Security Sector*. Before the World Bank, he worked and lived for more than a decade in the West Bank and Gaza and then Cambodia as a human rights lawyer, and for seven years with the United Nations in Somalia, Sudan, and the Great Lakes region. He then worked for two years with the UK government as senior conflict adviser, managing the Africa Conflict Prevention Fund. He has a background in criminal and human rights law, including a master's in international law from the London School of Economics, and is an adjunct professor and an adviser for the Mid-Atlantic Innocence Project and the Oxford Research Group.

Deborah Isser is lead governance specialist at the World Bank. Her focus is on the political economy of development and institutions that deliver basic services, justice, and security. She has led operations and analytical work in more than 15 countries in Africa, East Asia and Pacific, and the Middle East. She is coauthor of the *World Development Report 2017: Governance and the Law*, was program manager of the Justice for the Poor program, and was the focal point for fragile and conflict-affected states. Previously, she worked at the United States Institute of Peace, directing projects on legal pluralism and land conflict. She was senior policy adviser at the Office of the High Representative in Bosnia and Herzegovina and special adviser on peacekeeping at the United States Mission to the United Nations. She is the editor and author of several reports, articles, and book chapters on law, justice, and development. She is adjunct faculty at the Georgetown University Law Center and the George Washington University Law School. She received degrees from Harvard Law School, the Fletcher School of Law and Diplomacy, and Columbia University and was judicial clerk to The Honorable Justice Dalia Dorner of the Supreme Court of Israel.

Indhira Santos is a senior economist at the World Bank. She was part of the *World Development Report 2016: Internet for Development* team. Currently she is part of the Social Protection and Jobs Global Practice, based in Europe and Central Asia. Before the World Development Report assignment, she worked in the Europe and Central Asia Region. She specializes in labor market issues and skills development for employment. Previously, she worked on similar issues in the South Asia Region. She joined the World Bank in 2009 through the Young Professionals Program. Between 2007 and 2009, she was a research fellow at Bruegel, a European policy think tank in Brussels. She was a researcher at the economic research center of PUCMM University and worked for the Ministry of Finance. She has also worked for the Central Bank of Turkey. She holds a PhD in public policy from the Kennedy School of Government at Harvard University, with a specialization in economic development and public economics.

Michael Watts is Chancellor's Professor of Geography Emeritus and Co-Director of Development Studies at the University of California, Berkeley, California, where he taught for 40 years. He served as the Director of the Institute of International Studies at Berkeley from 1994 to 2004, and he was Director of

Social Science MATRIX from 2019–2020. He has held visiting appointments at the Smithsonian Institution and in Bergen, Bologna, and London. He served on the Board of Advisors of a number of nonprofit organizations, including Food First and the Pacific Institute, and he was Chair of the Board of Trustees of the Social Science Research Council. He is a member of the British Academy. He was named as a Guggenheim fellow in 2003; he was awarded the Victoria Medal by the Royal Geographical Society in 2004 and the Berlin Prize by the American Academy in Berlin in 2016. He is currently a fellow at the Swedish Collegium for Advanced Study in Uppsala, Sweden. He received his bachelor's degree from the University College London and his PhD from the University of Michigan.

Abbreviations

COVID-19	coronavirus
CSO	civil society organization
GDP	gross domestic product
GPSA	Global Partnership for Social Accountability
IEG	Independent Evaluation Group
SAR	special administrative region
UPs	union parishads
WDR	World Development Report

Overview

Introduction

Although some Sub-Saharan African countries are catching up to higher-income countries, many are falling behind despite their best efforts and those of the development community. Since their independence, a number of African countries have faced state-building and governance challenges, sometimes in the context of widespread political turbulence, civil conflict, military rule, and state failure, which has resulted in unevenness of national state capacity (asymmetrical state capabilities that vary across sector, scale of government, and over time), weakened political settlements, and ineffective civil society. The COVID-19 (coronavirus) pandemic could exacerbate these challenges and lead to the emergence of new ones from the socioeconomic effects of containment measures.

To explain current development outcomes and inform reforms, an increasing number of development partners are integrating sociopolitical framings into their strategies and programs. Development policy of the 1980s and 1990s often focused on liberalization, privatization, and austerity, aimed at reducing or limiting the size and scope of the state. These reforms were later criticized for their shortcomings, which spurred a rethinking of the approach to state-building and development. The *World Development Report 2017: Governance and the Law,* for example, argues that "policies that should be effective in generating positive development outcomes are often not adopted, are poorly implemented, or end up backfiring over time" (World Bank 2017, 2), and that the radically uneven character of public policy formulation, implementation, and enforcement is a matter of governance, namely, "the process through which state and nonstate actors interact to design and implement policies within a given set of formal and informal rules that shape and are shaped by power" (World Bank 2017, 3).

One particular sociopolitical framing attracting attention is based on the "social contract." Within the World Bank, for example, a recent report by the Independent Evaluation Group identified 21 Systematic Country Diagnostics that "use a social contract framing to diagnose and explain complex development challenges such as entrenched inequalities, poor service delivery, weak institutions, and why decades of policy and institutional reforms promoted by external development actors could not fundamentally alter countries' development paths" (IEG 2019, 7). The reason for this phenomenon is that social contracts relate to (1) the literature on the nexus between politics, power relations, and development outcomes, while (2) also bringing into focus the instruments that underpin citizen-state relations and foster citizen voice. Social contracts as a framing tool also directly speak to many contemporary development trends such as the policy-implementation gap, the diagnostic of binding constraints to development, fragility and conflict, taxation and service delivery, and social protection.

In Sub-Saharan Africa, however, an explicit treatment of social contracts has been largely absent from the development discourse. Over the past four or five decades, a complex and sophisticated body of scholarship from Africa has addressed the challenges of state-building and governance, sometimes against the backdrop of widespread political turbulence, civil conflict, military rule, and in some instances, something approaching state collapse. However, an explicit social contract lens has most often been missing. The lack of centrality of social contract theory in explaining Africa's recent history and development is perhaps not surprising given the theory's European roots and the need to "reinterpret" and adapt critical elements to some of the particular features present in African states.

With this in mind, this report seeks to lay the foundation for a unified framework for applying a social contract framing to development policy and using it to analyze the nature of social contracts in the region. To this end, the work makes a significant effort to set up a practical framework to allow the wide applicability of a social contract lens to relevant development challenges in specific sectors, countries, or regions in the continent. In doing this, the report—and the broader research program on which it rests—aims to address one of the critical limitations of the use of social contract diagnostics at the World Bank so far, that is, the lack of a formal conceptual framework or shared understanding of what the term means. The report, hence, focuses on the process by which social contracts are forged in the region, how they change over time, and how a more in-depth understanding of social contracts can help inform reform efforts. This approach stands in contrast to a normative approach that details the desirable content for the social contract in particular areas.

Main Messages

The key messages from this report are as follows:

- Africa's progress toward shared prosperity requires looking beyond technical policies to understanding how power dynamics and citizen-state relations shape the menu of implementable reforms. A social contract lens can help diagnose constraints, explain outbreaks of unrest, and identify opportunities for improving outcomes.

- Social contracts can be understood as "a dynamic agreement between state and society on their mutual roles and responsibilities." Social contracts can be evaluated on three "compasses": (1) process—how formal and informal bargaining mechanisms mediate civil and state interests and capabilities; (2) outcomes—the extent to which they deliver inclusive developmental policies and outcomes; and (3) resilience—the extent to which they are responsive to and aligned with citizen expectations. The interactions between these three dimensions of the social contract are illustrated in figure O.1.

Figure 0.1 Social Contracts Conceptual Framework

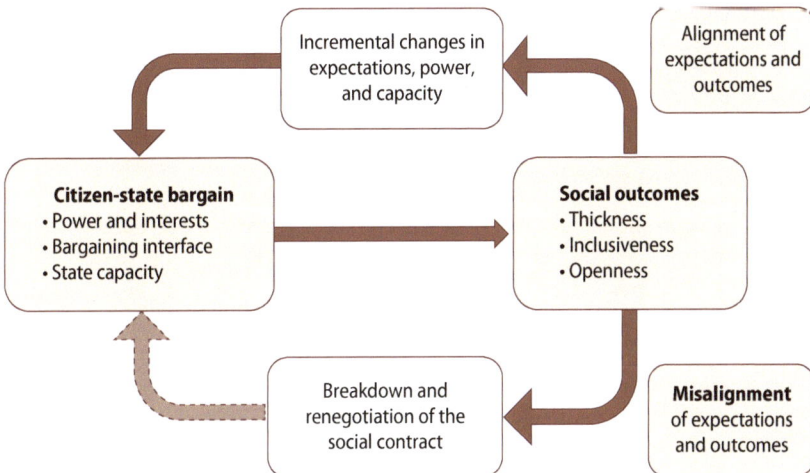

Sources: Based on Cloutier (2021) and OECD (2009) definition of social contracts.
Note: Thickness refers to the involvement of the state in providing services and public goods and in the redistribution of income and wealth (for example, education, health, social protection, or public infrastructure).

- To understand social contract dynamics in a country, region, or sector, measurement is critical, combining quantitative and qualitative tools to understand the deeper structural and sociopolitical factors that shape social contracts. Measurement also allows for a more granular study of social contracts at subnational and sector-specific levels. The report offers an indicator framework that can be used to measure key dimensions of each of the three social contract compasses.

- Although social contracts in Africa are both heterogeneous and dynamic, a number of common factors affect the three compasses: (1) processes of state formation and how these processes have shaped political settlements; (2) the strong role of nonstate authorities—religious traditional, military, and others—in mediating the relationship between citizens and the state; (3) electoral politics and the role of patronage and clientelism; (4) demographics of largely dispersed rural populations, a small middle class, and a limited independent private sector; and (5) natural resource and aid dependency.

- In recent years several African countries have experienced significant opportunities for renegotiation of the social contract, some successful and some less so. In some cases, this renegotiation took the form of constitutional or electoral moments (the Democratic Republic of Congo, The Gambia, Kenya, Malawi, Togo); in others, economic shocks, anger over corruption, and ethnic exclusion triggered large-scale protests and demands for deeper change, sometimes succeeding in ousting heads of state (Ethiopia, South Africa, Sudan, Zimbabwe). In all cases it was civil capacity—mass mobilization sustained over long periods—that created the possibility of reshaping social contracts.

- Adopting a social contract lens has significant implications for engagement by the World Bank and other external partners:

  o *Diagnostics.* The conceptual and empirical framework presented in this report can complement technical diagnostics by focusing on the sociopolitical aspects that are often the reason for chronic policy failure and may hold clues for reform opportunities. This framework can be applied at the national, subnational, sectoral, and issue-specific levels. The World Bank should further invest in new forms of both quantitative and qualitative data that are relevant to social contracts, including disaggregation of citizen perceptions and trust, to gain an understanding of the role of nonstate authorities and how sector-specific policies affect and are affected by the prevailing contract.

o   *Strategy.* The framework can provide consistency and concreteness in the use of social contract language and in how World Bank strategy can reflect the opportunities—and pitfalls—of its engagement with respect to local bargaining dynamics. This process involves self-awareness of how international actors such as the World Bank can unintentionally skew civil and state bargaining capacity and affect different dimensions of the social contract.

o   *Operations.* Operations should aim to strengthen government systems in ways that institutionalize mechanisms for effective civil bargaining, implying, for example, shifting from upstream public financial management reforms to engagement at the points at which government and citizens interact for service delivery. Sectoral projects should be careful not to create parallel systems that undermine citizen-state accountability.

References

Cloutier, M. 2021. "Social Contracts in Sub-Saharan Africa: Concepts and Measurements." Policy Research Working Paper, No. 9788, World Bank, Washington, DC. Washington, DC. http://documents.worldbank.org/curated/en/205501633362482731/Social-Contracts-in-Sub-Saharan-Africa-Concepts-and-Measurements.

IEG (Independent Evaluation Group). 2019. *Social Contracts and World Bank Country Engagements: Lessons from Emerging Practices.* Washington, DC: World Bank.

OECD (Organisation for Economic Co-operation and Development). 2009. "Concepts and Dilemmas of State Building in Fragile Situations: From Fragility to Resilience." OECD Journal on Development (9): 3. https://doi.org/10.1787/journal_dev-v9-art27-en.

World Bank. 2017. *World Development Report 2017: Governance and the Law.* Washington, DC: World Bank.

Chapter 1

Social Contracts in Sub-Saharan Africa: A Research Program

Introduction

Despite significant gains in the fight against poverty and tremendous continental heterogeneity, the Africa region continues to lag across development indicators. Although the incidence of extreme poverty fell from 54 percent in 1990 to 41 percent in 2015, persistently high fertility rates led to an absolute increase of Africans living on less than US$1.90 a day from 278 million to 413 million in that same time frame. By 2030 extreme poverty is expected to be an exclusively African phenomenon. African countries account for 24 of the 25 lowest scores on the Human Capital Index 2020 (World Bank 2020). Trailing other regions, energy access is at 37 percent; only 5 percent of agricultural land is irrigated; adult literacy is at 58 percent; and Africa's share of global foreign direct investment has hovered around 3 percent for the past decade (Zeufack et al. 2020).

In many states, delivery of public goods and services remains wanting, and the expected dividends from shifts to multiparty democracy in most parts of the continent have failed to yield either economic dynamism or enhanced state capability. The skills gap with other regions is increasing. The pace of structural transformation is slow, and the move out of agriculture is to a large extent into low-productivity and vulnerable informal jobs. More than 50 percent of the world's conflicts are also in Africa, while the region has only 16 percent of the global population (United Nations and World Bank 2018; World Bank 2017); large swaths of the continent suffer from the devastating effects of large-scale internal displacement, refugee flight, and economic out-migration.

Explanations for Africa's poor performance and persistent challenges are myriad, but the World Bank has generally focused on the issue of policy, positing that by adopting and implementing the "right policies" African states can break out of poverty traps. But the mixed record of decades of policy advice and technical assistance requires us to look more deeply at the underlying factors that explain policy uptake and outcomes in different contexts. The charge for this study was to use the lens of social contracts to explore these challenges and identify implications for World Bank engagements.

This approach builds on the increased attention paid to social and political economy factors that gained further traction with the publication of the *World Development Report 2017: Governance and the Law*. That report argues that "policy-making and policy implementation do not occur in a vacuum. Rather, they take place in complex political and social settings, in which individuals and groups with unequal power interact within changing rules as they pursue conflicting interests" (World Bank 2017, 29). Who bargains, who is excluded, and what rules shape the nature of the bargain determine the selection and implementation of policies and, consequently, their impact on development outcomes. Simply stated, policies and outcomes tend to reflect the interests of those with greater power.

The social contract angle focuses on a particular dimension of this power dynamic: that between citizens and the state. It hypothesizes that a healthy social contract, in which state policies reflect the demands and expectations of society, leads to more stable, equitable, and prosperous outcomes relative to those that do not. It also draws attention to the nature of the citizen-state bargaining process and the factors that shape and mediate the interests that are represented and the capabilities of delivering on expectations. The study, therefore, focuses on the process by which social contracts are forged in the region, how they change over time, and how a more in-depth understanding of social contracts can help inform reform efforts. This approach stands in contrast to a normative approach that details the shortcomings and desirable content for social contracts without grappling with the realities that shape them.

The onset of the COVID-19 (coronavirus) pandemic in 2020 has placed a spotlight on these relationships as states face the public health threat, impacts of containment, and the global slowdown, putting additional stress on state and citizen relations. The outbreak has set off the first recession in the region in 25 years, with growth forecast between −2.1 percent and −5.1 percent in 2020 from a modest 2.4 percent in 2019. In turn, the pandemic shock has seriously affected relations between rulers and the ruled and highlighted the importance of trust and legitimacy along with technical capability (Khemani 2020). These impacts are occurring against a backdrop of increased protest over the past decade (Branch and Mampilly 2015; LeBas 2013; Mueller 2018), now compounded by lockdown measures (Ramdeen 2020), which is hampering the effectiveness of addressing pandemic outcomes.

In this context, this report provides a timely synthesis of findings from a regional research program that engaged a multidisciplinary group of scholars to explore the role of social contracts in explaining and addressing contemporary

African development challenges. The research program involved multiple layers of engagement and exploration of the topic, including the following:

- *Working paper series.*[1] Two framing papers focused on developing a working framework and an understanding of social contracts in Africa and one aimed at quantitatively characterizing social contracts in the region. In addition, six country studies (Cameroon, Niger, Nigeria, Senegal, Somalia, and South Africa), four thematic studies (two on human rights, one on taxation, and one on social protection), and four spotlights on issues of operational importance to the region were undertaken.

- *Seminars and presentations.*[2] Seminars and presentations were held that included academics and researchers to obtain a clear set of concepts around the social contract. An authors' seminar revolved around thematic and country case studies. A number of presentations were given by members of the wider social contract team to World Bank staff, including by Michael Watts, professor emeritus, Berkeley; Leonard Wantchekon, professor, Princeton University; and Belinda Archibong, associate professor, Barnard College. Presentations were also made to wider audiences on specific themes of the report.

- *Applications of the social contract regional study.* The team supported country teams in selected Systematic Country Diagnostics and country strategy work to bring in the social contract lens (for example, in Malawi, Nigeria, Somalia, South Africa, Sudan, and Tunisia) as well as its application to gaining an understanding of how to support development at the local level (Haiti).

Chapters 2 and 3 of this report address one of the critical limitations of the use of social contract analysis to date, that is, the lack of a conceptual framework or shared understanding of the term. Chapter 2 explores the evolution and application of social contract terminology within the literature of African politics and development on the one hand and within World Bank discourse on the other. Building on this discussion, chapter 3 sets forth a working definition of social contracts and a conceptual framing for identifying the critical components and factors that characterize social contracts in specific contexts. This framing is accompanied by a qualitative and quantitative methodology for assessing social contracts and comparing them across space, time, and different sets of development challenges. It offers overarching findings from the application of the quantitative framework broadly across the continent.

Chapters 4 and 5 apply the conceptual and quantitative framework to a series of country case studies and thematic spotlights. These studies are not meant to be comprehensive accounts; one important aspect of this report's framing is that countries cannot be reduced to a single social contract but are characterized by multiple, overlapping spaces of citizen-state bargaining. The examples serve to illustrate how a social contract lens can shed light on broad development trajectories as well as to identify productive entry points.

Chapter 6 sets out practical implications of the study for World Bank strategic and operational engagement in the region. Given the inherently contextual nature of social contracts the report does not provide prescriptive recommendations; rather, the focus is on how to apply social contract analysis from a methodological perspective as well as a strategic one. It examines how, on the one hand, it is overreaching to suggest that the World Bank can seek to shape social contracts in client countries. Yet, on the other, by injecting resources, expert advice, and support into contested spaces, Bank interventions will inevitably have an impact on internal bargaining dynamics. Accordingly, a social contract lens and theory of change is critical to making informed choices about engagement.

Notes

1. The working papers include Ahmad and Irwin (2019), Cloutier (2021), Bentley (2019), Dreier et al. (2020), Fisiy (2019), Konte (2019), Okunogbe (2020), Ordor (2020), Tidjani Alou (2019), and Watts (2018a, 2018b, 2019).
2. Those academics and researchers participating included Aisha Ahmad, associate professor, University of Toronto; Belinda Archibong, associate professor, Barnard College; Kristina Bentley, senior researcher, University of Cape Town; Mamadou Diouf, professor, Columbia University; James Habyarimana, associate professor, Georgetown University; Tim Kelsall, senior research fellow, Overseas Development Institute; Maty Konte, associate professor, University of Maastricht; Peter Lewis, professor, Johns Hopkins University; Erin McCandless, associate professor, University of Witwatersrand; Lisa Mueller, associate professor, Macalester College; Cyril Obi, director of African Peacebuilding, New York; Ada Ordor, associate professor, University of Cape Town; Danielle Resnick, senior research fellow, International Food Policy Research Institute; Abdi Samatar, professor, University of Minnesota; Mahaman Tidjani Alou, professor, Abdou Moumouni University; Leonard Wantchekon, professor, Princeton University; and Michael Watts, professor emeritus, University of California, Berkeley.

References

Ahmad, A., and I. Irwin. 2019. "Somalia Case Study." Unpublished, World Bank, Washington, DC.

Bentley, K. 2019. "Background Paper on Human Rights, the Social Contract and Development." Unpublished, World Bank, Washington, DC.

Branch, A., and Z. Mampilly. 2015. *Africa Uprising: Popular Protest and Political Change.* London: Zed Books Ltd.

Cloutier, M. 2021. "Social Contracts in Sub-Saharan Africa: Concepts and Measurements." Policy Research Working Paper Series, World Bank, Washington, DC.

Dreier, S., A. Lagrange, M. Lake, and A. Porisky. 2020. "Social Protection and the Social Contract." Unpublished, World Bank, Washington, DC.

Fisiy, C. 2019. "Social Contract and State Effectiveness in Cameroon." Unpublished, World Bank, Washington, DC.

Khemani, S. 2020. "An Opportunity to Build Legitimacy and Trust in Public Institutions in the Time of COVID-19." World Bank, Washington, DC.

Konte, M. 2019. "Senegal Case Study." Unpublished, World Bank, Washington, DC.

LeBas, A. 2013. *From Protest to Parties: Party-Building and Democratization in Africa.* Oxford: Oxford University Press.

Mueller, L. 2018. *Political Protest in Contemporary Africa.* Cambridge, U.K.: Cambridge University Press.

Okunogbe, O. 2020. "The Relationship between the Social Contract and Support for Taxation in Africa." Working Paper. Unpublished. World Bank, Washington, DC.

Ordor, A. 2020. "Human Rights as a Tool to Strengthen the Social Contract in Africa." Unpublished, World Bank.

Ramdeen, M. 2020. "Social and Political Protests, Exacerbated by the Covid-19 Pandemic, on the Increase in Africa." *Accord,* July 8, 2020.

Tidjani Alou, M. 2019. "L'Etat et les contrats sociaux au Niger: Eléments d'approche." Unpublished, World Bank, Washington, DC.

United Nations and World Bank. 2018. *Pathways for Peace: Inclusive Approaches to Preventing Violent Conflict.* Washington, DC: World Bank.

Watts, M. 2018a. "Political Settlements in Nigeria." Unpublished, University of California, Berkeley.

Watts, M. 2018b. "States, Societies and Social Contracts: Understanding State Capacity, Political Orders and Civic Society Engagement in Africa." Unpublished, University of California, Berkeley.

Watts, M. 2019. "States, Societies and Citizenship: The Changing Social Contract in Post-Apartheid South Africa." Unpublished, University of California, Berkeley.

World Bank. 2017. *World Development Report 2017: Governance and the Law.* Washington, DC: World Bank.

World Bank. 2020. *The Human Capital Index 2020 Update: Human Capital in the Time of COVID-19.* Washington, DC: World Bank.

Zeufack, A. G., C. Calderon, G. Kambou, C. Z. Djiofack, M. Kubota, V. Korman, and C. Cantu Canales. 2020. *Africa's Pulse,* No. 21 (April), World Bank, Washington, DC.

Chapter 2

Tracing Social Contract Theory

Social Contract Theory and Development in Africa[1]

The origins of social contract theory can be traced as far back as antiquity. Plato's Republic describes a social arrangement for what the philosopher saw as a perfect society. The field has also been a staple of Euro-American political theory since the seventeenth century, with philosophers such as Thomas Hobbes, John Locke, and Jean-Jacques Rousseau discussing the role and purpose of the state and of the ruler.

The social contract has been understood in different ways throughout history. The classical theorists, such as Hobbes, Locke, and Rousseau, were interested in the question of the origin and legitimacy of states and rulers. For them, the social contract is an agreement whereby individuals consent to lay down their rights and subject themselves to the coercive power of the state, subject to everyone making a similar commitment. For modern social contract theorists, such as Rawls, the existence of the state is often taken as a given and the focus is on identifying the social institutions and policies that reflect justice as a foundational virtue of a society or that try to optimize some function of the state. These social contract theories can also be seen through the lens of the conditions under which negotiation over the social contract takes place. *Contractarians* argue that agents are driven by the rational pursuit of personal interest, whereas *contractualists* see agents as concerned with reaching a reasonable agreement on universal principles of justice that are capable of governing society.

The first explicit engagements with social contracts in development theory emerged in the 1990s and early 2000s from different directions in different regions. In the Middle East, the collapse of oil prices and the structural adjustment programs of the 1980s brought to the fore the need to rethink social contracts based on handouts to maintain social peace. In Latin America and East Asia in the 1990s and 2000s, direct engagement with the social contract emerged around social welfare politics, examining the changing forms of social protection in "incipient welfare states." A third engagement took place as scholars attempted to explain social stability in the 1980s in the former Soviet Union and the Eastern Bloc through the existence of an "implicit social contract" that citizens should remain quiescent to the degree that the party-state provided secure jobs and services, subsidized housing, and (controlled) consumer goods. These early engagements laid the groundwork for the proliferation of social contract talk across regions, institutions, and sectors. Social protection contracts (Carbone and Pellegata 2017; Devereux 2004; Hickey 2008), taxation contracts (Bräutigam, Fjeldstad, and Moore 2008), social accountability contracts (Hickey and King 2016; Houtzager 2003), peacebuilding and postconflict (fragility-resilience) social contracts (Leonard and Samantar 2011; McCandless 2018a and b), and socioeconomic compacts (Acemoglu and Robinson 2012) all became part of the development lexicon during the 2000s.

In contrast, the language of social contracts was largely absent from the expansive body of Africanist research on the postcolonial state and its colonial and precolonial legacies. Over the past four or five decades a complex and sophisticated body of scholarship from Africa has addressed the challenges of state-building and governance, sometimes against the backdrop of widespread political turbulence, civil conflict, military rule, and in some instances, something approaching state collapse; however, the explicit social contract lens has often been missing. The lack of centrality of social contract theory in explaining Africa's recent development is perhaps not surprising given the need to "reinterpret" and adapt critical elements of the theory to some of the particular features present in African states.

Many of the assumptions that underlie the modern approach to social contract theory, such as an emphasis on the dichotomy of state and citizens, or even taking the existence of a state for granted, do not translate seamlessly to the study of Africa. On one side, the historical context of colonial legacies (precolonial empires, settler states, peasant- or resources-fueled economies, forms of direct and indirect rule) and the paths to independence (liberation movements, negotiated settlement) shaped the African state. On the other side, the theory was not adapted for some important aspects of the context. Mamdani (1996) emphasizes certain of these aspects, including the continued role of so-called customary law and institutions and chiefly powers, the tensions between "indigenes" and "settlers" (newcomers) in multi-ethnic states, the incomplete character of citizenship, and the entrenched tensions and political separation between town and country. These historical approaches powerfully established the path-dependencies of forms of colonialism, the coexistence of multiple and overlapping forms of authority (chieftainship, local government, religious authority), and the enduring significance of culture (ethnicity and religion) in understanding political change.

None of this is to suggest that questions of state capacity or questions of political authority or legitimacy were ignored—quite the contrary.[2] For example, a thread emerged to examine how society or social structures had or had not "captured" the state (this is the heart of Hyden's influential book *Beyond Ujamaa* [1980] on the "economy of affection") (see also de Sardan 1999). Some of the recent scholarship on African states (for example, Bayart 2006; Bayart, Ellis, and Hibou 1997, 2009; Mbembe 1990) examines the privatization of the state, the criminalization of some state apparatuses, and the rise of "private indirect government."

Meanwhile, the social contract as a body of theory was for the most part undeveloped.[3] It is in the past decade that a very different picture has emerged. The fact that social contract theory as a tool of analysis has contemporary currency is borne out in the frequency with which the term appears in contemporary development literature (analytical and prescriptive), not least in the case of Africa.[4] One of the first explicit treatments of social contracts focused on food security. De Waal's (1996) research addresses what he called "antifamine contracts" and was in large measure a response to Sen's (1993) important work on starvation. De Waal emphasizes the complex forms of inclusion and exclusion associated with these contracts and the fact that donors ("the humanitarian international") sometimes circumvented the antifamine contracts and state authority.

Social contract concepts have also been explicitly used in relation to three arenas of growing salience in African development. One is taxation in Africa—"no representation, no taxation" is a core component of contractual thinking—and the notion that a very basic measure of state capacity is total revenue collection. A book on taxation in Africa (Prichard 2015) shows how the bargaining between citizens and governments over tax collection varies across the continent, but reliance on taxation has in fact increased responsiveness and accountability by expanding the political power wielded by taxpayers.

The second arena in which social contract language has been central to policy debate is postconflict reconstruction and peacebuilding (for a review, see McCandless 2018a, 2018b; NOREF 2016; UNDP 2014).[5] The question of so-called fragility, resilience, and endemic conflict, which encompasses everything from civil wars to the rise of militias, transnational gangs, and terror groups, centers on the legitimacy of states and their despotic powers (or limits thereon). The rise of nonstate armed groups is almost by definition a marker of a fractured or contested social contract.

The third arena is that of social protection, where Hickey et al. (2018) argue that variation in degrees of coverage and embeddedness results from the contestation and negotiation between political elites, voters, bureaucrats, and transnational actors. The formation of "policy constituencies" around social protection, that is to say the embedding of some social contractual principles whereby social protection can become a "structural linkage" suturing states and citizens through forms of bargaining and agreement, is already evident at low levels in some countries, as with the long-standing if minimalist Public Welfare Assistance Scheme in Zambia (Harland 2014). Conversely, the danger is that external interventions, as de Waal (1996, 1997, 2000) found in the 1990s around food security, can undermine the development of a social contract.

For social contract theory to add value to the broader study of political economy and development in Africa, it must be able to accommodate the critical features of African state formation and citizen-state relationships and allow for a robust empirical, rather than normative, analysis. This chapter next discusses how social contract theory has been applied within the World Bank in other regions before turning to a conceptual framing adapted for the African region.

Social Contract Theory at the World Bank

In the 1980s and early 1990s, the World Bank's approach to development involved many reforms (liberalization, privatization, and austerity) aimed at reducing or limiting the size and scope of the state. These reforms were later criticized for their shortcomings, which spurred a rethinking of the approach to state-building and development. This effort led to the increased realization that many intangible factors have an impact on the success of development programs, contributing to the rise of "inclusive liberalism" (Craig and Porter 2006) and an emphasis on good governance, accountability, and state capacity. The World Bank's work includes many examples of this shift in development philosophy. The *World Development Report 2011: Conflict, Security, and Development* (World Bank 2011) on postconflict recovery addresses the need to construct "inclusive-enough coalitions" and to engage with informal institutions and patronage networks in the attempt to acquire "broader societal legitimacy" and "proactive communication…to build public understanding and support" (World Bank 2011, 124). Central to the report's model is the grounding of postconflict transitions in fairness and the "political inclusion of all citizens." The *World Development Report 2017: Governance and the Law* (World Bank 2017) directly addresses the importance of the law and the power bargains that surround policies and programs. The report argues that the World Bank needs to integrate an analysis of these intangible factors when designing projects. These reports, while not framed in terms of the social contract, contain critical components of social contract theory (legitimation, agreement and negotiation, pact arrangements, and so forth).

In the past decade, the World Bank has increased its use of the concept of social contract. Former World Bank President Robert Zoellick first referred to social contracts and development in 2009 following the global financial crisis, and it became a more central plank of World Bank discourse in the wake of the Arab Spring in 2011 and 2012. In the exposition of its twin goals of ending extreme poverty and boosting shared prosperity, the World Bank calls for "social contracts within each country demanding that the poor be a priority in the policy environment that supports the growth process" (IEG 2019, 1). Recent examples (box 2.1) show the growing use of the social contract concept in the World Bank's engagement, as in the 2015 Middle East and North Africa strategy and the 2018 Europe and Central Asia Region flagship report, *Toward a New Social Contract: Taking On Distributional Tensions in Europe and Central Asia* (Bussolo et al. 2018). The 2015 Middle East and North Africa strategy is one of the World Bank's most ambitious attempts to translate social contract diagnostics into country operations. According to the Independent Evaluation Group, anchoring the Middle East and North Africa strategy around social contract renewal created new policy reform opportunities and improved the World Bank portfolio's coherence and targeting of lagging regions. The 2018 Europe and Central Asia Region flagship report (Bussolo et al. 2018, 3) explicitly states that "the report put an economic interpretation on the concept [of social contract]" and defines it as the "individuals' agreement for the broad outline of economic policies if the outcomes of these policies coincide with their preferences." Redefining social contracts as an economic equilibrium helped justify the World Bank's foray into social contract renewal and its recommendations for what social contracts should look like. However, stripping social contracts of their sociopolitical dimensions could be seen as problematic because of its reductivism (IEG 2019).

BOX 2.1

Uses of the Social Contract across the World Bank

Social contract terminology in the World Bank has been found useful at the regional level to reflect on major trends and to call for reform. In the wake of the global financial crisis, the Arab Spring, and increasing concerns about conflict and inequality, the World Bank and several other organizations have increasingly adopted the concept of the social contract at the country and regional levels when analyzing development outcomes and possible reforms. In this context, social contracts are often used as a tool with which to describe the functioning (or lack of functioning) of specific aspects of the relationship between states and citizens. However, in the absence of a common conceptual framework and guidance on its applicability, the notion of the social contract then takes on different meanings and is applied very differently across the board. Two prominent examples follow:

Social contract in the Middle East and North Africa. According to the 2015 World Bank strategy for the region, before the Arab Spring the prevailing social contract was based on stable public jobs, subsidies, and decent services for citizens while the state retained autocratic control with little accountability. The strategy argued that social

(continued next page)

Box 2.1 (continued)

contract had been abrogated given that the constraints on state resources had undermined the ability of the state to deliver its side of the bargain, leading to the Arab Spring (and the resurgence of radical Islam). This created the need for—and opportunity to—redefine the social contract to address grievances and rebuild legitimacy, based on enabling private sector–led jobs, improving services, and increasing citizen voice and accountability.

Social contract in Europe and Central Asia. In the 2018 report *Toward a New Social Contract: Taking On Distributional Tensions in Europe and Central Asia* (Bussolo et al. 2018), the social contract is seen as an equilibrium between distributional outcomes generated by market forces, modified by public policies and people's preferences. Preferences are grounded in values of distributional equity and entitlements, but the preferences are increasingly out of line with the outcomes produced by market forces and public policies. This, in turn, is leading to questions of generational shifts, youth frustration, income inequality, labor market polarization, and market-driven distributional tensions, giving rise to right-wing authoritarian populism and racist xenophobia. What is needed to regain equilibrium, the report argues, is a focus on distributional equity, and hence a redefinition of the social contract.

Despite the increased use of the term "social contract" in World Bank analytical and operational work, the lack of a common framework is seen as a limitation for truly embedding notions of the citizen-state relationship in analyses and policy recommendations (IEG 2019). For example, in many cases reports and diagnostics find that social contracts are "broken," and they recommend their "renewal" or "rebuilding" but without offering a satisfying definition of what it means for the social contract to be broken or how it can be rebuilt.

The 21 Systematic Country Diagnostics examined by the Independent Evaluation Group (IEG) (2019) apply uneven rigor to the use of "social contract," leading to ambiguity over how social contract diagnostics can guide actions. Despite adopting a social contracts approach in their diagnostics, 45 percent of the Systematic Country Diagnostics sampled did not provide a definition of the concept. Another 23 percent used a state-focused definition that exclusively emphasized the role of the public sector to deliver public goods and services, provide social protection (social safety nets and subsidies), and create an environment conducive to growth. In contrast, 9 percent had a citizen-focused definition that emphasized greater citizen engagement as central to increasing long-term growth, as well as economic and social inclusion for peace and social stability. Finally, less than a quarter provided a more nuanced definition that combined, to some extent, the roles (and rights) of, and relationships between, the state, citizens, and other stakeholder groups.

The IEG report concludes that "social contract diagnostics are useful analytical innovations with relevant operational implications" (IEG 2019, 32). However, the report notes that "currently the World Bank has no formal conceptual framework or shared understanding of social contracts, leading to uneven quality of use" (IEG 2019, 12).

Hence, this regional study examining social contracts in Africa aims to fill that gap and provide a conceptual framework and shared understanding of the term. By definition, this must be a working understanding that may change over time subject to more analysis, but a conceptual framing is important in identifying the critical components and factors that can influence government and partner policy and investments.

Notes

1. This section is derived from Watts (2018) (a background paper for the Africa Social Contract study), which contains a more detailed discussion of the evolution of social contract theory, its use in development literature and Africa specifically, and a proposed framework for its application.
2. For a detailed account of the multiple strands of literature on African political economy and their engagement with historical dependencies and concepts of power, incentives, and collective action, see Watts (2018).
3. There are, however, three important exceptions: two are specific to two wildly different state formations (Senegal [Babou 2016] and South Africa [Heller 2017; Sisk 1995], and the other (Nugent 2010) provides a typology of various "African state logics" to grasp how the state mediates the production and reproduction of inequalities.
4. A Google Scholar search of social contracts and development theory in Africa since 2014 yields 17,000 citations. See Addison and Murshed 2001; Alston et al. 2013; German Development Institute 2016; Kaplan 2014; World Bank 2018.
5. As a UNDP report (McCandless 2018a, 11) on fragile and conflicted states notes, "A resilient national social contract is a dynamic agreement between state and society, including different groups in society, on how to live together, how power is exercised and how resources are distributed. It allows for the peaceful mediation of conflicting interests and different expectations and understandings of rights and responsibilities (including with nested and/or overlapping social contracts that may transcend the state) over time, and in response to contextual factors (including shocks, stressors and threats), through varied mechanisms, institutions and processes."

References

Acemoglu, D., and J. Robinson. 2012. *Why Nations Fail: The Origins of Power, Prosperity and Poverty*. New York: Crown.

Addison, T., and S. M. Murshed. 2001. "From Conflict to Reconstruction: Reviving the Social Contract." Discussion Paper 2001/48, UNU/WIDER, Helsinki.

Alston, L. J., M. A. Melo, B. Mueller, and C. Pereira. 2013. "Changing Social Contracts: Beliefs and Dissipative Inclusion in Brazil." *Journal of Comparative Economics* 41 (1): 48–65.

Babou, C. A. 2016. "Negotiating the Boundaries of Power: Abdoulaye Wade, the Muridiyya, and State Politics in Senegal, 2000–2012." *Journal of West African History* 2 (1): 165–88.

Bayart, J. F. 2006. L'Etat en Afrique: la politique du ventre. Paris: Fayard.

Bayart, J. F., S. Ellis, and B. Hibou. 2009. *The Criminalization of the State in Africa.* Indiana: Indiana University Press.

Bayart, J. F., S. Ellis, and B. Hibou. 1997. La criminalisation de l'Etat en Afrique, Éditions Complexe.

Bräutigam, D., O-H. Fjeldstad, and M. Moore, eds. 2008. *Taxation and State-Building in Developing Countries: Capacity and Consent.* Cambridge, U.K.: Cambridge University Press.

Bussolo, M., M. E. Dávalos, V. Peragine, and R. Sundaram. 2018. *Toward a New Social Contract: Taking On Distributional Tensions in Europe and Central Asia.* Washington, DC: World Bank.

Carbone, G., and A. Pellegata. 2017. "To Elect or Not to Elect: Leaders, Alternation in Power and Social Welfare in Sub-Saharan Africa." *Journal of Development Studies* 53 (12): 1965–87.

Craig, D. A., and D. Porter. 2006. *Development beyond neoliberalism? Governance, Poverty Reduction and Political Economy.* London: Routledge.

de Sardan, O. 1999. "A Moral Economy of Corruption in Africa?" *Journal of Modern African Studies* 37 (1): 25–52.

Devereux, S. 2004. "Transformative Social Protection." Working Paper 232, Institute of Development Studies, Brighton, U.K.

De Waal, A. 1996. "Social Contract and Deterring Famine: First Thoughts." *Disasters* 20 (3): 194–205.

De Waal, A. 1997. *Famine Crimes: Politics and the Disaster Relief Industry in Africa.* Oxford: James Currey/IAI.

De Waal, A. 2000. *Democratic Political Process and the Fight against Famine.* IDS Working Paper 107. Sussex: Institute of Development Studies, University of Sussex.

German Development Institute. 2016. "A New Social Contract for MENA (Middle East and North Africa) Countries: Experiences from Development and Social Policies." German Development Institute conference, Bonn, December 5–6.

Harland, C. 2014. "Can the Expansion of Social Protection Bring about Social Transformation in African Countries? The Case of Zambia." *European Journal of Development Research* 26: 370–86.

Heller, P. 2017. "Development in the City." In *States in the Developing World*, edited by M. Centeno, A. Kohli, D. J. Yashar, and D. Mistree, 309–38. Cambridge, U.K.: Cambridge University Press.

Hickey, S. 2008. "Conceptualizing the Politics of Social Protection in Africa." In *Social Protection for the Poor and Poorest: Concepts, Policies and Politics*, edited by A. Barrientos and D. Hulme. Basingstoke, U.K.: Palgrave MacMillan.

Hickey, S., and S. King. 2016. "Understanding Social Accountability: Politics, Power and Building New Social Contracts." *Journal of Development Studies* 52 (8): 1225–40.

Hickey, S., T. Lavers, M. Nino-Zaruza, and J. Seekings. 2018. "The Negotiated Politics of Social Protection in Sub-Saharan Africa." Working paper 2018/34, UNU-WIDER, Helsinki.

Houtzager, P. 2003. "Introduction: From Polycentrism to the Polity." In *Changing Paths: International Development and the New Politics of Inclusion*, edited by P. Houtzager and M. Moore, 1–31. Ann Arbor: University of Michigan Press.

Hyden, G. 1980. *Beyond Ujamaa in Tanzania: Underdevelopment and an Uncaptured Peasantry.* Portsmouth, NH: Heinemann Books.

IEG (Independent Evaluation Group). 2019. *Social Contracts and World Bank Country Engagements: Lessons from Emerging Practices.* Washington, DC: World Bank.

Kaplan, S. 2014. "Social Covenants and Social Contracts in Transitions." Report, NOREF (Norwegian Peacebuilding Resource Center).

Leonard, D., and M. Samantar. 2011. "What Does the Somali Experience Tell Us about the Social Contract and the State?" *Development and Change* 42 (2): 559–84.

Mamdani, M. 1996. *Citizen and Subject: Contemporary Africa and the Legacy of Late Colonialism.* Princeton: Princeton University Press.

Mbembe, A. 1990. Pouvoir, violence et accumulation, Politique Africaine.

McCandless, E. 2018a. *Forging Resilient Social Contracts: A Pathway to Preventing Violent Conflict and Sustaining Peace. Summary Findings.* Oslo: United Nations Development Programme.

McCandless, E. 2018b. *Reconceptualizing the Social Contract: In Contexts of Conflict, Fragility and Fraught Transition.* Johannesburg: Wits School of Governance.

NOREF (Norwegian Peacebuilding Resource Center). 2016. *Engaged Societies, Responsive States: The Social Contract in Situations of Conflict and Fragility.* New York/Oslo: United Nations Development Programme.

Nugent, P. 2010. "States and Social Contracts in Africa." *New Left Review* 63: 35–68.

Prichard, W. 2015. *Taxation, Responsiveness and Accountability in Sub-Saharan Africa: The Dynamics of Tax Bargaining.* Cambridge, U.K.: Cambridge University Press.

Sen, A. 1993. "Capability and Well-Being." In *The Quality of Life*, edited by M. Nussbaum and A. Sen, 30–53. Oxford: Clarendon Press.

Sisk, T. 1995. *Democratization in South Africa: The Elusive Social Contract.* Princeton: Princeton University Press.

UNDP (United Nations Development Programme). 2014. *Shaping the State through Social Contracts in Situations of Conflict and Fragility.* Conference and Experts Meeting report. New York: UNDP.

Watts, M. 2018. "States, Societies and Social Contracts: Understanding State Capacity, Political Orders and Civic Society Engagement in Africa." Unpublished, University of California, Berkeley.

World Bank. 2011. *World Development Report 2011: Conflict, Security, and Development.* Washington, DC: World Bank.

World Bank. 2017. *World Development Report 2017: Governance and the Law.* Washington, DC: World Bank.

World Bank. 2018. "An Incomplete Transition: Overcoming the Legacy of Exclusion in South Africa. Republic of South Africa Systematic Country Diagnostic." World Bank, Washington, DC.

Chapter 3

Social Contracts in Africa: A Conceptual and Empirical Framework

Social Contract Definition and Conceptual Framework

One of the main objectives of this report is to propose a conceptual and empirical framework with which to analyze the nature of social contracts and their link to development outcomes. The report adopts the following simple definition of a social contract: "a dynamic agreement between state and society on their mutual roles and responsibilities" (OECD 2009, 77). This definition highlights the three core aspects of the social contract: the citizen-state bargain, the social outcomes, and the resilience of the contract. First, by emphasizing that social contracts are agreements, although often implicit ones, the definition introduces the idea that some form of bargaining is involved and therefore that the parties to the contract have bargaining positions and bargaining powers. This concept relates closely to the framework set out in *World Development Report* (WDR) *2017: Governance and the Law* (World Bank 2017), which defines governance as the processes through which state and nonstate actors interact to design and implement policies within a given set of formal and informal rules, and is shaped by, and in turn shapes, power relations (box 3.1). Second, when the definition mentions the roles played by the actors and their responsibilities toward each other it implies that the policies that result from the citizen-state bargain influence the observed and experienced social outcomes. In other words, a country's policies, programs, and laws represent the contents of the social contract and have an impact on how resources and rents are allocated within society. Third, by recognizing that the agreement is dynamic, the definition also highlights that social contracts are not static. They are continuously renegotiated, they are subject to self-reinforcing cycles and feedback loops, and their evolution is highly endogenous and path-dependent. Social contracts can also break down; therefore, a framework for understanding social contracts needs to consider how they evolve over time and their level of resilience.

BOX 3.1

World Development Report 2017 and Social Contracts

The conceptual understanding of social contracts presented in this report is grounded in the ideas of the *World Development Report* (WDR) *2017: Governance and the Law* (World Bank 2017). The 2017 WDR argues that many development challenges are less about identifying and crafting robust policies, legislation, or laws and more about the political challenges of adopting, implementing, and enforcing them (the so-called implementation gap) (see also DFID 2010). Social contract thinking reinforces the notion that framing poor governance and state deficits as the failure to follow best practice, or as a lack of political will or state capacity, has a constricted view of what constitutes policy, the policy arena, and reform initiatives. It also largely ignores how formal and informal institutions that distribute power or the different ways of ordering power shape the rules of the game (Chatterjee 2004; Slater 2011). Policies do not occur in a vacuum; rather, "they take place in complex political and social settings in which individuals and groups with unequal bargaining power interact within changing rules as they pursue conflicting interests" (World Bank 2017, 29).

The framework developed in the WDR 2017 connects to social contract theory through the notion of citizen-state bargaining. The distribution of power, who holds power, and the power asymmetries among different actors and agents are key elements of the ways in which the policy arena (both the rules of the game and the outcomes of the game) actually functions and whether and what quality of public goods and services are delivered. How effective, in the broadest sense, policies are with regard to their design and capability to achieve development goals depends on key institutions and their three core functions: enabling credible commitment, inducing coordination, and enhancing cooperation. The existence and operation of these functions, however, will be shaped by, and possibly compromised by, the ordering of power and the dominant power asymmetries. That is to say, they are influenced by the types of regime, by the existence (or not) of political parties and electoral systems, and by the more or less organized forms in which social actors such as the military, political parties, the executive branch of government, business lobbies, the judiciary, organized labor, and civil society groups populate the policy bargaining process. The patterns and mechanisms of elite bargaining, citizen engagement, and popular struggle within the policy space shape the likelihood that the core institutional functions will be obtained. These elements are recognized in the following description (OECD 2009, 77, emphasis added):

> The social contract ... emerges from the interaction between a) *expectations* that a given society has of a given state; b) *state capacity* to provide services, including security, and to secure revenue from its population and territory to provide these

(continued next page)

Box 3.1 (continued)

services (in part a function of economic resources); and c) *élite will* to direct state resources and capacity to fulfil social expectations.

It is crucially mediated by d) the existence of *political processes through which the bargain between state and society is struck*, reinforced and institutionalized.

Finally, e) *legitimacy* plays a complex additional role in shaping expectations and facilitating political process. Legitimacy is also produced and replenished—or, conversely—eroded by the interaction among the other four factors...

Taken together, the interaction among these factors **forms a dynamic agreement between state and society on their mutual roles and responsibilities**—a social contract.

Approaching the social contract from a citizen-state bargain perspective is useful for many reasons. First, it directly connects with many of the ideas suggested in the WDR 2017, which can be adapted and extended. Second, it suggests a straightforward way of explaining some of the observed variation in outcomes across different contexts. Third, it gives the framework some predictive power given that changes in bargaining powers should naturally lead to changes in bargain outcomes. The conceptual framework of this report examines three aspects of social contracts, referred to as "compasses":

- *Process*, that is, what is the nature of the bargaining space for social contracts? Drawing on WDR 2017, this compass seeks to provide an understanding of the ways in which formal and informal bargaining mechanisms mediate the range of state and nonstate interests and capabilities.

- *Outcomes*, that is, what is the substantive outcome of the bargain? What does the state commit to deliver in return for compliance, stability, staying in power, and so on?

- *Resilience*, that is, to what extent is the outcome responsive to and aligned with citizen expectations (or to what extent is it misaligned and counter to expectations), how open is the dialogue between citizens and the state, and how does this in turn lead to changes or breakdowns in the bargaining dynamic?

As illustrated in figure 3.1, these compasses form a feedback loop of self-reinforcing cycles.

Figure 3.1 Social Contracts Conceptual Framework

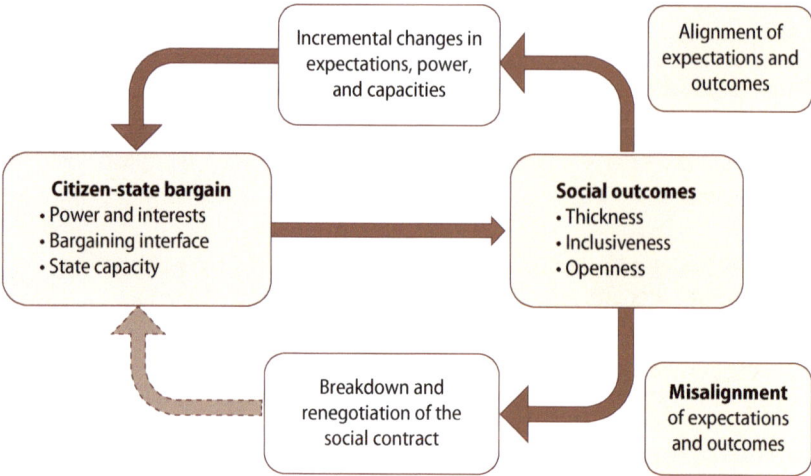

Sources: Based on Cloutier (2021) for this report and OECD (2009) definition of social contracts.
Note: Thickness refers to the involvement of the state in providing services and public goods and in the redistribution of income and wealth (for example, education, health, social protection, or public infrastructure).

Compass 1: Process, The Citizen-State Bargain

The citizen-state bargain is a complex process involving many heterogeneous groups of actors with different interests interacting through diverse channels and means. Citizens are not homogeneous and coalesce in multiple overlapping coalitions and groups. Some groups are very broad and loosely organized, for example, the youth or the middle class. Other groups are narrower and can form interest groups, such as workers in a specific sector forming a union. Finally, elites can be understood as the smallest groups, usually consisting of a very powerful individual or family. By "powerful," this report means the group's capacity to influence decision-makers' willingness to act, or in other words its bargaining power.[1] These groups can change over time and are constantly interacting with each other and with the state. These interactions are mediated through channels and mechanisms such as elections and protests, or through intermediaries such as the press, social media, lobbies, political leaders, and others.

This report posits that one of the most important forms of bargaining power for inclusive and equitable development is the one that encompasses the broadest coalitions of citizens. This is referred to as "civil capacity" and represents the capacity of citizens to resolve the collective action problem and to present a united front to make demands of the state and to hold it accountable for its commitments. Civil capacity aims to capture a variety of dimensions, including (1) citizen mobilization, that is, how engaged citizens are in public forums and how involved in politics they are; (2) citizen organization, referring to how well-organized the civil society is, for example, the number of civil society organizations and their role and influence in society; and (3) citizen cooperation, that is, the absence of fractionalization or group grievances among citizens.

Although civil capacity is a relatively new term, there is a large literature covering related concepts and their role in the social order of societies. The concept of social capital, in particular, has played an important part in clarifying the workings and role of society in critical processes such as democracy or addressing collective action problems (Putnam 2000; Putnam, Leonardis, and Nanetti 1993). Social capital emphasizes the functioning of social groups through interpersonal relationships, a shared sense of identity, understanding and norms, shared values, trust, cooperation, and reciprocity; the concept of civic capital focuses on how effectively this social capital can be leveraged in the citizens' relationship with the state (Guiso, Sapienza, and Zingales 2016). Some evidence indicates that, across countries, elements affecting "social cohesion," such as income inequality and ethnic fractionalization, endogenously determine institutional quality, which, in turn, causally determines growth (Easterly, Ritzen, and Woolcock 2006). In Africa, social cohesion has been found to partly explain a diverse set of outcomes, including agricultural innovation (van Rijn, Bulte, and Adekunle 2012) and health outcomes (Story 2013).

A second critical dimension in the citizen-state bargain of the social contract framework is state capacity. State capacity determines the size of the pie being divided among the groups of citizens and the state itself. It covers three domains: (1) deployment of state authority, that is, the capacity to enforce the monopoly on violence and laws over the whole territory; (2) resource mobilization and taxation; and (3) the ability of the state bureaucracy to spend these resources efficiently.[2] Administrative or bureaucratic capacity is a growing topic in the development literature, including at the World Bank's Bureaucracy Lab.[3] The evidence on the importance of civil capacity continues to grow, but existing indications make it clear that it is critical for the delivery of public goods and, hence, to the trust in and workings of the social contract. In Nigeria, for example, improving management practices was found to be an important determinant of bureaucrats' capacity to deliver services (Rasul and Rogger 2016).

Importantly, the framework captures both formal and informal relations. Social contracts in African settings typically involve formal and informal relations, they are more or less explicit and implicit, they express complex forms of sociopolitical inclusion and exclusion, they are sometimes fragmented and sometimes cohesive, and they encompass complex and overlapping forms of authority.[4] The informal networks of power outside of formal political channels—customary and religious forms of authority—and "external forces" (from multilateral development agencies, to peacekeeping forces, to changing development ideologies and practices, to global market shocks) provide local context and have fundamentally shaped the construction and reproduction of contracts. Social contracts are dynamic and changing too, and even where there is a "balance of social forces" producing periods of stability, the fact remains that critical junctures and ruptures punctuate the trajectories of all African social contracts.

Compass 2: Social Contract Outcomes

The citizen-state bargain, through the multiple, iterative, and dynamic processes described in figure 3.1, affects (and is affected by) social contract outcomes, thereby affecting development outcomes. Many potential social contract outcomes could be measured, but this report focuses on three categories: thickness, inclusiveness, and openness.

- *Thickness* refers to the involvement of the state in providing services and public goods and in the redistribution of income and wealth (for example, education, health, social protection, or public infrastructure). This dimension can be seen as a typology based on a "thin" to "thick" spectrum in which a thin social contract would be one of economic laissez-faire and minimal involvement of the state in the economy whereas a thick social contract would be characterized by a more involved state. This aspect is related to the size of the government in the economy, for example, as measured by public expenditure versus gross domestic product (GDP), but nuanced by the distribution of that expenditure by sector (for example, in health or education as opposed to in the military) or by final beneficiaries (for example, the rich, the middle class, or the poor).

- *Inclusiveness* measures whether the social contract is geared toward benefiting the broad population or a select few. It is based mainly on two pillars: (1) fair opportunity, social inclusion, and absence of inequality; and (2) the existence of the rule of law, meaning the absence of abuse of powers such as corruption and clientelism. In this outcome there is also a spectrum, ranging from an extractive social contract to an inclusive one. An inclusive social contract would involve fairness of opportunity and an important level of socioeconomic mobility for the general population. A social contract could be extractive through corruption, clientelism, and barriers to entry (in business or in politics) or through social exclusion of certain minorities or vulnerable groups. An extractive social contract would exhibit the kind of rent extraction and extractive institutions described in the work of Acemoglu, Johnson, and Robinson (2005) and Acemoglu and Robinson (2012).

- *Openness* refers to how open the state is to diverging opinions and its use of repression to silence criticisms. This outcome ranges from a repressive social contract to a responsive one. An open social contract would feature freedom of the press and of expression, whereas a repressive social contract would feature censure, political killings, and torture. Openness also introduces the different mechanisms, interfaces, and intermediaries that are involved in the bargaining over and implementation of the social contract. An important literature related to this dimension covers the choice of political system and the roles of elections. For example, an important field of research (for example, Acemoglu et al. 2019) discusses whether democracy is linked to economic outcomes such as growth. These considerations of democracy and elections are one of the possible forms that the citizen-state bargain can take and, therefore, are deeply connected to the social contract. Although a social contract outcome, openness is closely associated with the responsiveness of the state to changes in citizens' power and interests. Without sufficient openness, peaceful renegotiation of the social contract is more difficult, which increases the likelihood of a breakdown. For this reason, openness is included in the Resilience compass when mapped.

Compass 3: Resilience and Dynamism

In this framework, expectations are central to the dynamic nature of social contracts, in particular, the alignment (or misalignment) of citizens' expectations with their perceptions of the social contract outcomes. Elements of trust and legitimacy are fundamental.[5] The alignment dimension can also be expressed as a spectrum from a misaligned social contract to an aligned one. Citizens' conceptions of what an aligned social contract is changes from country to country, depending on history, culture, and many other factors. One of the propositions of this framework, substantiated by empirical analysis (Cloutier, 2021), is that citizens' expectations are also linked to their perceptions of the state's capacity and their own civil capacity. Citizens are mostly aware of the kind of service delivery they can expect given the state's capacity or what kind of protections of their rights they can expect given their civil capacity to hold the state accountable. When applied to the alignment dimension, one could imagine citizens in a country with little civil capacity or state capacity expecting little from the state, which could, for example, make a thin, extractive, and repressive social contract be perceived as aligned. Alignment and openness, jointly, are indications of the resilience of a social contract.

This third compass is linked to the dynamic nature of social contracts. The main implication of this dynamic nature is that all the elements in the framework are endogenous and interdependent. State and civil capacities influence social contract outcomes, but they are also themselves products of prevailing outcomes. An example illustrating this endogeneity could be to imagine an increase in the thickness of a social contract through an expansion of the delivery of public education. This expansion could then lead to a more educated population composed of citizens that can then better organize, increasing their civil capacity over time, and hence increasing their capacity to demand more education services from the state in a self-reinforcing cycle of incremental change.

As an alternative to incremental change, history is full of examples of revolutions and critical juncture moments when social contracts can be renegotiated drastically within the span of a few years or when a complete breakdown leads to years of social unrest and civil war. The end of apartheid in South Africa (as illustrated in the corresponding case study [Watts 2019]) is a clear example of such a critical juncture that led to a drastic renegotiation of the social contract; the Nigerian civil war of the 1960s and the revolts against term duration reforms in Burundi, Guinea, and Togo are examples of situations in which the social contract broke down, leading to social unrest.

In the framework, this dynamism is captured by presenting two possible paths for the evolution of the social contract. The path taken depends on the alignment dimension, which captures how aligned citizens' perceptions are with their expectations. First, when the level of alignment is above a certain threshold, meaning that citizens' perceptions of social outcomes are relatively in line with their expectation, the evolution of the agreement is incremental. This would be the case of the education example given above. Second, when the alignment has been decreasing for a certain time or when a sudden change in one of the social contract dimensions generates a large shock in alignment, the social contract can potentially break down, meaning that it cannot continue on the same path. In this situation, renegotiation is possible but only if there is an open dialogue such as through pathways measured by the openness dimension. If open dialogue is not possible, conflict and unrest could be unavoidable.

The dynamic aspect of social contracts also means that social contracts can be very path dependent. Prevailing social contracts are influenced by a range of factors outside the critical pillars discussed here, including the historical context of the country, the culture of its citizens, and economic conditions, among many others. However, as discussed in the next section, an analysis of the critical social contract dimensions in the region, the case studies and sectoral spotlights, and the empirical analysis conducted by the authors of the background papers support the claim that the citizen-state bargaining process remains an important determinant of social contracts and possesses significant predictive and explicative power. The framework's predictive capability can be useful for analyzing exogenous changes to the capacity of a country coming from either the intervention of outside actors such as the World Bank or the introduction of new technologies, which can dramatically impact capacity. For example, such an interpretation has been proposed to link how higher social media penetration affected the organization of social movement during the Arab Spring (Howard et al. 2011).

Measuring the Compasses: An Indicator Framework

Moving from this constellation of features and concepts to a measurable framework requires a narrower focus that takes into account empirical limitations.[6] The dimensions of the three compasses identified in the framework do not exist in a vacuum, but need to be interpreted in light of the historical, structural, and ideational context that shapes the particular possibilities in a given country and around a given issue. This kind of analysis requires qualitative and quantitative methods drawing from multiple disciplines. Chapter 4 discusses some of the common characteristics that shape African social contracts and illustrates them in country case studies and sectoral applications. Here the report offers an approach to measuring some of the core dimensions of the conceptual framework using available cross-country indicators.

Social contracts themselves are not observable or explicitly described anywhere, making it difficult to characterize their nature or to measure their evolution. The usual approaches to circumventing this difficulty involve finding a proxy for the quality of the overall compact (Hoogeveen 2018) or focusing on measuring specific outcomes related to the social contract, such as inequality, prosperity, or stability. The approach taken in this report tries to combine the two methods. The framework identifies specific dimensions of the contract to be measured and classifies them as either inputs of the social contract bargain or as outcomes. The framework then offers a theoretical lens with which to interpret these individual dimensions in a way that informs the overall compact such as in the former method. It is this integrative and systematic view that allows critical dimensions of the social contract to be measured.

This report proposes an empirical methodology for measuring the previously identified dimensions of the social contract. Using indicators from multiple sources (including expert assessments and self-reported surveys),[7] a means of mapping six dimensions from the conceptual framework—state and civil capacity, on the bargaining side; inclusiveness, thickness, and openness on the outcome side; and alignment on the resilience and dynamic evolution side—was developed. Readily available indicators from multiple sources were used; a detailed methodology of their construction as well as summary statistics can be found in annex 3A.[8] The measurements presented in the remainder of the report are calculated using that methodology for 2015.

The summary statistics for the indicators used as inputs to the framework suggest that countries in Africa span the entire range of the indicators' spectrum. Averages for African countries tend to be lower than for the rest of the developing world for income per capita and taxes per capita, while being higher than the other regions on indicators describing the quality of civil society and social safety nets. Most important, the minimum and maximum ranges show the large heterogeneity of social contracts in Africa. The region features countries that do better along most dimensions than other middle-income or lower-income countries, as well as countries that score at the bottom of almost all categories, along with mixed-case countries. Among the top scorers are Botswana, Mauritius, Namibia, Senegal, and Seychelles; at the lower range are mostly countries experiencing or coming out of conflict, such as the Democratic Republic of Congo, Somalia, and Sudan.

Indicators of social contracts for Africa (and globally) support the validity of the model for the region (Cloutier, 2021). As predicted by the framework, both higher civil capacity and higher state capacity are strongly correlated with better social contract outcomes. This result supports the core assumptions that the citizen-state bargain is at the center of the formation of social contracts in Africa. Furthermore, there are also strong correlations between better social contract outcomes and a closer alignment of expectations with perceived outcomes. A less intuitive prediction of the model is that perceptions of these outcomes should matter more for alignment than expert-based measures of these outcomes. This prediction is empirically supported by showing that the perceived level of outcomes from citizen surveys better predicts alignment than more expert-based measures. This fact suggests that expectations and perceptions play a major role in determining citizens' satisfaction with the social contract. Taken together, this evidence suggests that the framework has explicative power.

Following the conceptual framework, the report focuses on three key social contract compasses to characterize the social contract: citizen-state bargain, social contract outcomes, and resilience. Figures 3.2 through 3.4 present the aggregate indexes for each country for the dimensions included in each of the social contract pillars. In the figures, the red lines represent the median scores for African countries for each dimension, and the red dots identify the six countries that are covered in the case studies for this report. Each country score is calculated using the methodology presented in annex 3A. The list of country acronyms can be found in annex 3B.

First, both civil and state capacity are mapped. Lack of capacity can be a constraint to improvements in the social contract, for example, when a state does not have the resources or know-how necessary to implement reforms or programs, or when citizens struggle to mobilize with sufficient strength to sway policy. Figure 3.2 indicates a strong correlation between civil capacity and state capacity. A possible explanation for this phenomenon is the kind of feedback loop that was previously discussed and which relates to the strong endogeneity of the dimensions; external factors can also drive both civil and state capacity. For example, an increase in civil capacity could shift the social contract toward improved access to education, which could, in turn, feed back into higher civil capacity through a better educated population, but also increase state capacity

Figure 3.2 Civil and State Capacities across Africa

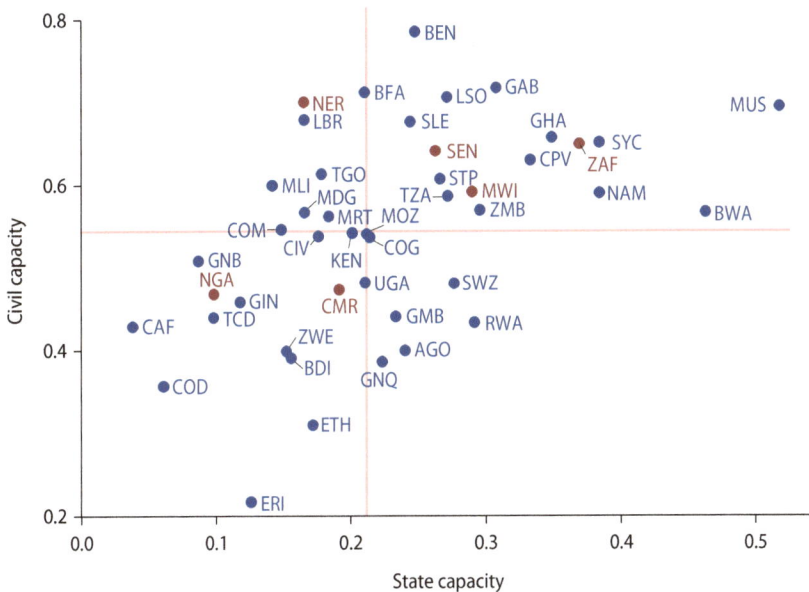

Source: World Bank calculations based on data from the University of Gothenburg's Varieties of Democracy Index, the Fragile States Index of the Fund for Peace, the Economist Intelligence Unit, and the World Bank's Worldwide Governance Indicators.
Note: The score for each dimension is the equally weighted average of the scores for each of its subdimensions scaled to a [0,1] interval. The red lines are the median value for each dimension.

because the state could hire better-trained bureaucrats. Similarly, improvements in the quality of the education system require a certain level of state capacity to recruit and pay the teachers as well as some level of civil capacity so that the state devotes the resources to it. Given the endogeneity and feedback loops mentioned, it is likely that countries in the southwest and northeast quadrants are in equilibrium.

Despite the high correlation between state and civil capacity, a number of countries also present mixed pictures. Countries in the northwest quadrant exhibit high levels of civil capacity for their levels of state capacity, whereas countries in the southeast quadrant have low levels of civil capacity given their state capacity. One clear example of a mixed-capacity country is Niger, which has a particularly high civil capacity level for its level of state capacity. The context and sociohistorical origins of this situation are discussed in the Niger case study (Tidjani Alou 2019). How this mixed capacity, and the resulting social contracts, evolve in these contexts is less clear. In particular, there can be cases in which high state (civil) capacity can help increase low civil (state) capacity;

however, there can also be cases in which the opposite happens and low state (civil) capacity pulls down high civil (state) capacity.

Second, figure 3.3 characterizes the degree to which social contracts in the region are thick and inclusive. In the figure, thicker and more inclusive social contracts are situated in the northeast quadrant whereas thinner and more extractive social contracts are in the southwest quadrant. The positive correlation seen in the figure is consistent with the framework's assumption that the citizen-state bargain to some extent explains both outcomes. Of particular interest are countries in which these social contract outcomes are not that strongly correlated. Countries in the northwest quadrant have high levels of inclusiveness given their level of thickness, while countries in the southeast quadrant have relatively high levels of thickness given their level of inclusiveness. In some cases, these outliers could present opportunities and entry points for potential policy dialogue. For example, a country might have gone through a period of high citizen mobilization and political will around a social project to improve health services, which boosts thickness. It is possible that this mobilization of state and civil capacity also established favorable conditions for an equivalent reform program to reduce corruption or increase the fairness of the justice system, which would boost the inclusiveness of the social contract.

Figure 3.3 Social Outcomes across Africa

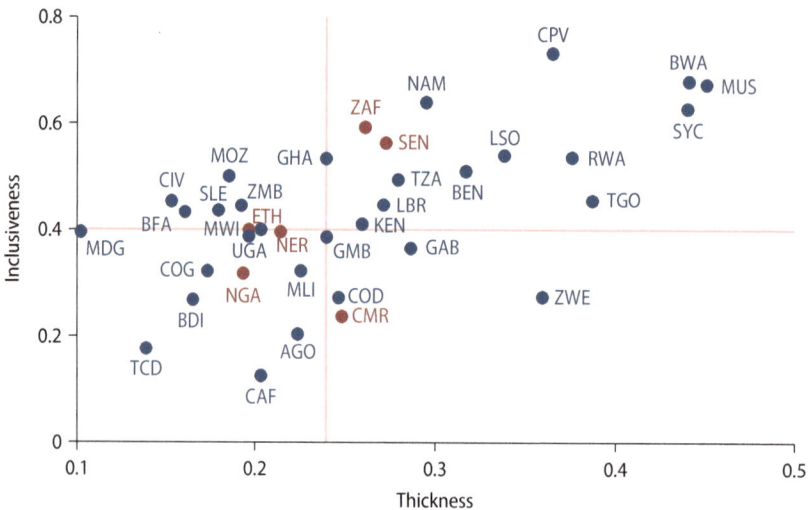

Source: World Bank calculations based on data from Afrobarometer, the University of Gothenburg's Varieties of Democracy Index, Fraser Institute, Freedom House, and Transparency International.
Note: The score for each dimension is the equally weighted average of the score for each of its subdimensions scaled to a [0-1] interval. The blue color lines are the median value for each dimension.
Thickness refers to the involvement of the state in providing services and public goods and in the redistribution of income and wealth (for example, education, health, social protection, or public infrastructure).

Third is a focus on resilience, mapping countries along the two dimensions of openness and alignment (figure 3.4). The resilience of the social contract can contribute to anticipating or explaining social unrest and breakdowns of the social contract based on the hypothesis that a misalignment between citizens' perceptions of social policies and their expectations could be resolved through peaceful renegotiation only if there is space for open dialogue. Without sufficient openness from the state, the social contract could struggle to adjust to changing expectations, perceptions, preferences, or bargaining powers, and a growing misalignment could eventually lead to a breakdown, conflict, or social unrest. In figure 3.4, data points in the southwest quadrant are characterized by low levels in both dimensions and could be associated with low-resiliency social contracts. Countries in the northeast quadrant have higher-than-median scores for alignment and openness, which could be associated with resilience. Botswana, not surprisingly, is in this quadrant, being the oldest democracy in Africa and having the lowest perceived corruption in the region for decades in an environment of fast economic growth. Countries in the northwest quadrant have openness above the median but are below the median with respect to alignment. Finally, countries in the southeast quadrant have below-median openness levels but above-median alignment levels and countries in the

Figure 3.4 Resilience in Social Contracts across Africa

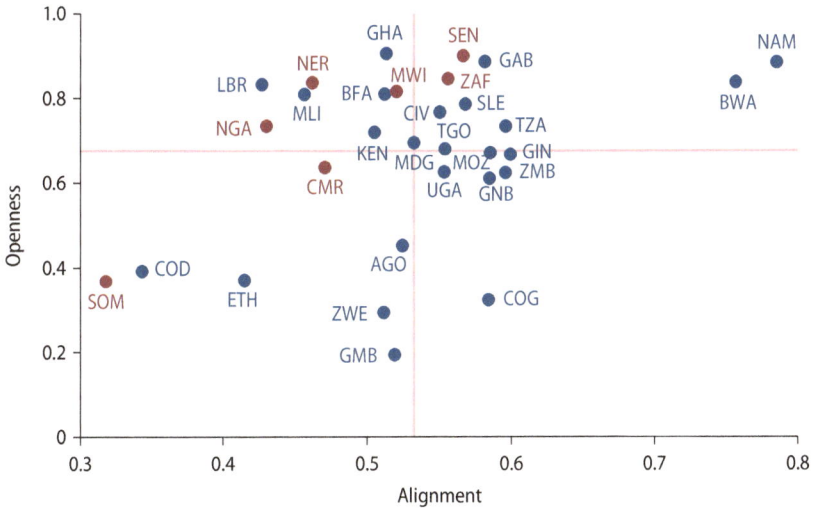

Source: World Bank calculations based on data from the University of Gothenburg's Varieties of Democracy Index, the World Bank's Worldwide Governance Indicators, and the PRS Group.
Note: The score for each dimension is the equally weighted average of the score for each of its subdimensions scaled to a [0,1] interval. The blue lines are the median value for each dimension.

southwest quadrant have below median openness and alignment. Somalia is in this quadrant and, as the case study prepared in this work program indicates (Ahmad and Irwin 2019), alignment and openness are both unsurprisingly low where the relationship between state and citizen is moderated by a number of actors that both substitute for and undermine the state.

The links between openness and alignment indicate possible self-reinforcing dynamics. The framework suggests that countries in the northwest quadrant would tend to move eastward and improve alignment because openness can lead to better-aligned policies when capacity is not a constraint. Likewise, countries in the southeast quadrant would tend to move westward with worsening alignment because the lack of openness would hinder the capacity of the social contract to adapt to changing conditions. Interestingly, both the northeast and southwest could be an equilibrium—in the absence of external shocks—because of self-reinforcing cycles. Comparing the positions of some of the countries in 2015 to their situation today offers some anecdotal support to the validity of the prediction.

Some important findings are suggested by this comparative analysis of social contract dimensions. First, there is wide heterogeneity between African nations across all dimensions. Acknowledging these differences is critical to understanding social contracts in Africa. Second, there is significant heterogeneity within countries on the compasses. Some countries score relatively well on all dimensions, but many have clear strengths and weaknesses that, notwithstanding feedback loops, can help identify policy entry points for reform. These feedback loops and reinforcing cycles can be positive if a country finds itself in a "high" equilibrium but can constitute poverty traps when in a "low" equilibrium. Potentially, development interventions could help nudge a country in a low equilibrium toward a different path.

The framework provides some additional insights.[9] First, it is clear that better social contract outcomes are strongly correlated with higher alignment scores, suggesting that citizens usually desire or expect thicker, more inclusive, and more responsive social contracts. Second, the best predictors of alignment of a social contract appear to be the perceptions of citizens, collected through perception surveys, rather than the expert-based measures of social contract outcomes. Finally, a key finding from this analysis is that state capacity without civil capacity is not sufficient to generate high levels of positive social contract outcomes. This finding has important operational implications that are particularly relevant for international development institutions that often focus most of their engagement on building state capacity through training and technical assistance and often invest less in building citizen capacity.

This empirical framework is most useful when it is combined with a multidisciplinary qualitative analysis. This approach helps address the data limitations described above while also having three additional advantages. First, as mentioned, the citizen-state bargain, albeit central, is not the only factor affecting social contracts. However, although external factors are not explicit in the framework, they can be introduced indirectly through their impacts on the critical dimensions of social contracts included in the framework. Second, this framework is applied at the national level; at the subnational level or in specific sectors, social contract dynamics can play out very differently. Although this level of granularity is difficult to implement quantitatively, the framework can be easily applied in a qualitative manner beyond the national level, as shown in some of the case studies (for example, Nigeria) and in the sector-specific spotlights. Third, and arguably most critically, the quantitative application of this framework needs to be combined with a qualitative and detailed analysis of intermediaries and bargaining mechanisms that frames the citizen-state relation in each context. The qualitative and country-specific nature of this aspect means it requires a country-by-country analysis as is done in the case studies prepared under the research program forming the basis of this report.

Annex 3A Empirical Methodology and Summary Statistics

This annex describes the empirical measurement strategy of the framework introduced in chapter 3. The process of constructing the measures for the 6 dimensions consists of identifying proxy indicators for the 14 subdimensions that compose them. These proxies come from readily available indicators from multiple sources. The main databases used as sources include the University of Gothenburg's Varieties of Democracy Index (V-DEM), the World Bank's Worldwide Governance Indicators, the Fragile States Index of the Fund for Peace, and the Afrobarometer surveys. The sources of the indicators for each of the subdimensions are presented in table 3A.1. The final score for each dimension is the equally weighted average of the score for each of its subdimensions, with all the indicators used as proxies scaled to a [0,1] interval. Table 3A.2 presents the summary statistics for all the underlying indicators used to measure the subdimensions.

The indicators used in the report are for 2015 and the sample size covers 178 countries. In the empirical analysis presented in this report, the data used are centered around 2015 but range from 2013 to 2017 because of limited availability of certain sources. The number of countries in the sample consists of a maximum of 178 countries for the global cross-section, with some countries missing for certain variables. When looking at perceptions-based surveys, the sample size is 29 countries in Sub-Saharan Africa because of the use of the Afrobarometer as the main data source.

The empirical methodology is subject to the usual empirical caveats and limitations. Both types of data sources (expert based and self-reported) come with their own biases and measurement errors. Another limitation of the empirical strategy comes from using secondary indicators as proxies; these secondary

Table 3A.1 Measuring the Social Contract in Africa: Indicators

Subdimensions	Data sources
Civil capacity	
Citizen organization	V-DEM
Citizen mobilization	V-DEM
Citizen cooperation	Fragile States Index
State capacity	
State authority	Fragile States Index
State resources	Economist Intelligence Unit
State efficiency	Worldwide Governance Indicators
Thickness	
Public goods	V-DEM; Afrobarometer
Social safety nets	Fraser Institute; Afrobarometer
Inclusiveness	
Equal opportunity	Freedom House; Afrobarometer
Absence of corruption	Transparency International; Afrobarometer
Openness	
Human rights	V-DEM; Afrobarometer
Freedom of expression and of the press	V-DEM; Afrobarometer
Alignment	
Civil compliance	Worldwide Governance Indicators; Afrobarometer
Popular support	The PRS Group; Afrobarometer

Source: V-DEM = Varieties of Democracy.

indicators have limited accuracy for reflecting the targeted subdimension. The variables included in the framework were selected based on both availability and accuracy criteria for the dimensions previously. The accuracy is imperfect, meaning that sometimes their scope is broader than the dimension they are meant to capture and other times it is narrower and does not fully capture the dimension. These limitations were addressed as much as possible by considering a large selection of data sources and many combinations of the indicators. New data sources and indicators are continuously being introduced, and the framework could gradually become more precise as they are integrated. A final caveat is that many additional aspects of social contracts could not be incorporated into the framework because of their qualitative nature or because they were too specific to a given context or country. An example of an aspect that could not be incorporated in the framework at the time is the subnational variation within a country of the different dimensions. Including this aspect would require a level of granularity in the data that would go beyond the scope of this report. A second example of a missing element concerns the intermediaries and bargaining mechanisms that frame the citizen-state relation.

Table 3A.2 Summary Statistics for the Empirical Framework

Variable	Non-SSA HIC					Non-SSA LIC and MIC					SSA				
	Obs.	Mean	Standard deviation	Minimum	Maximum	Obs.	Mean	Standard deviation	Minimum	Maximum	Obs.	Mean	Standard deviation	Minimum	Maximum
V-DEM Engaged Citizens	48	1.67	0.98	-1.08	3.18	82	0.57	1.18	-2.62	3.01	48	0.62	1.03	-1.49	2.98
V-DEM CSO Participatory Environment	48	1.27	1.11	-2.11	2.73	82	0.63	1.13	-3.01	2.26	48	0.94	0.93	-2.72	2.56
FSI Intergroup Grievances	50	4.46	1.65	1.30	9.70	75	7.20	1.41	3.90	10.00	48	6.56	1.97	3.70	10.00
FSI Security Apparatus	50	3.02	1.50	1.00	7.00	75	6.81	1.58	3.10	10.00	48	6.99	1.76	2.80	10.00
EIU Tax revenues per capita (PPP $)	51	1564594	831687	310524	4040800	76	284658	200105	9542	745811	46	131508	196398	8564	902675
WGI Government Effectiveness	47	1.18	0.59	-0.03	2.24	76	-0.42	0.61	-2.02	1.40	47	-0.81	0.68	-2.20	1.05
V-DEM Educational Equality	48	1.96	0.81	-0.58	3.18	82	0.08	1.14	-2.18	2.73	48	-0.35	1.11	-2.99	2.12
V-DEM Health Equality	48	2.16	0.69	0.40	3.79	82	0.13	1.16	-1.93	2.91	48	-0.48	1.08	-3.22	2.37
EFW Transfers and Subsidies	47	5.85	1.99	2.31	9.61	61	8.07	1.68	3.69	10.00	38	9.31	0.75	7.16	10.00
FH Personal Autonomy and Individual Rights	47	13.11	3.58	2.00	16.00	76	8.13	2.83	0.00	13.00	47	6.70	2.90	1.00	13.00
TI Corruption Perceptions Index	46	67.52	15.36	39.00	91.00	72	32.75	10.90	8.00	65.00	45	32.71	12.35	8.00	63.00
V-DEM Clientelism Index	48	0.90	0.13	0.35	0.98	82	0.63	0.25	0.02	0.97	48	0.58	0.27	0.07	0.96
V-DEM Physical Violence Index	48	0.83	0.26	0.13	0.98	82	0.61	0.27	0.02	0.96	48	0.67	0.24	0.02	0.94

(continued next page)

Table 3A.2 (continued)

Variable	Non-SSA HIC					Non-SSA LIC and MIC					SSA				
	Obs.	Mean	Standard deviation	Minimum	Maximum	Obs.	Mean	Standard deviation	Minimum	Maximum	Obs.	Mean	Standard deviation	Minimum	Maximum
V-DEM Freedom of Expression and Alternative Sources of Information index	47	0.67	0.58	−1.09	1.53	76	−0.51	0.86	−2.97	0.97	47	−0.55	0.84	−2.38	1.04
PRS Popular Support	49	2.18	0.35	1.00	3.00	58	2.01	0.51	1.00	3.50	32	2.13	0.38	1.50	3.00
AB Difficulty to obtain medical treatment	0					0					29	0.41	0.13	0.19	0.64
AB Difficulty to obtain public school	0					0					29	0.30	0.10	0.07	0.51
AB Handling improving living standards of the poor	0					0					28	0.28	0.11	0.08	0.66
AB Treated unequally	0					0					29	0.59	0.13	0.32	0.83
AB Corruption of government officials	0					0					29	0.40	0.13	0.21	0.70
AB How much fear, political intimidation	0					0					29	0.25	0.13	0.05	0.51
AB Free to say what you think	0					0					29	0.74	0.15	0.38	0.96

Sources: AB = Afrobarometer; EFW = Economic Freedom of the World (Fraser Institute); EIU = Economist Intelligence Unit; FH = Freedom House; FSI = Fragile States Index; PRS = The PRS Group; TI = Transparency International; V-DEM = Varieties of Democracy; WGI = Worldwide Governance Indicators.

Note: CSO = civil society organization; HIC = high-income countries; LIC = low-income countries; MIC = middle-income countries; Obs. = observations; PPP = purchasing power parity; SSA = Sub-Saharan Africa.

Annex 3B Country Codes

Table 3B.1 Country Codes

Country	Abbreviation	Country	Abbreviation
Angola	AGO	Madagascar	MDG
Benin	BEN	Malawi	MWI
Botswana	BWA	Mali	MLI
Burkina Faso	BFA	Mauritania	MRT
Burundi	BDI	Mauritius	MUS
Cameroon	CMR	Mozambique	MOZ
Cabo Verde	CPV	Namibia	NAM
Central African Republic	CAF	Niger	NER
Chad	TCD	Nigeria	NGA
Comoros	COM	Rwanda	RWA
Democratic Republic of Congo	COD	São Tomé and Príncipe	STP
Republic of Congo	COG	Senegal	SEN
Côte d'Ivoire	CIV	Seychelles	SYC
Equatorial Guinea	GNQ	Sierra Leone	SLE
Eritrea	ERI	Somalia	SOM
Eswatini	SWZ	South Africa	ZAF
Ethiopia	ETH	South Sudan	SSD
Gabon	GAB	Sudan	SDN
Gambia, The	GMB	Tanzania	TZA
Ghana	GHA	Togo	TGO
Guinea	GIN	Uganda	UGA
Guinea-Bissau	GNB	Zambia	ZMB
Kenya	KEN	Zimbabwe	ZWE
Lesotho	LSO		
Liberia	LBR		

Note: The country codes were provided in the dataset downloaded from the World Bank data catalog: https://datacatalog.worldbank.org/.

Notes

1. This is similar to the definition of the WDR 2017, which defines power as "the ability of groups and individuals to make others act in the interest of those groups and individuals and to bring about specific outcomes" (World Bank 2017, 3).
2. These three subindicators mirror the three dimensions of state capacity outlined in Hanson and Sigman (2013): extractive capacity, coercive capacity, and administrative capacity.
3. "Bureaucracy Lab," World Bank, https://www.worldbank.org/en/research/dime /brief/Bureaucracy-Lab.
4. See also the concept of political settlement in the body of work by Khan (2010).
5. Trust and legitimacy are terms that are often used in the literature, although in many different ways. For example, Fukuyama (1995) notes that trust can have two dimensions: trust in the state and trust in the government of the day. Trust in the state refers to the extent to which citizens believe that "the state" (in this case, the executive branch of the state) has the expertise, technical knowledge, capacity, and impartiality to make good judgments; that is, that it has an adequate number of people with the right training and skills to carry out the tasks they are assigned, and to do them in a timely and professional manner. Trust in the government of the day, in contrast, is more about trust in the politicians that form the government.
6. The first limitation is data availability. Perception surveys, in particular, are available for relatively few years, usually coming in the form of waves and for selected countries. All data sources also come with their own biases and measurement errors. Another limitation comes from the use of secondary indicators as proxies. The selected variables were the best that were available but are imperfect; sometimes they capture broader effects than desired and sometimes narrower effects. These limitations were addressed as much as possible by considering a large number of data sources and many combinations of the indicators. New data sources and indicators are continuously being created, and the framework could gradually become more precise as these sources are integrated. Country-specific work can also allow for better measurement in a number of cases.
7. Although expert assessments and self-reported surveys both attempt to measure the same thing, it is generally recognized that one of the biases that affects perception surveys is related to the subjectivity of the perceptions relative to the expectations of the surveyed population. Combining these two sources thus provides some information on the state of both perceptions and expectations of citizens, which is a critical element of social contracts.
8. Data sources and measurement strategy are described in more detail in the relevant background paper for this report: Cloutier (2021).
9. The evidence for these findings is more thoroughly discussed in the relevant background paper for this report (Cloutier, 2021).

References

Acemoglu, D., S. Johnson, and J. A. Robinson. 2005. "Institutions as a Fundamental Cause of Long-Run Growth." In *Handbook of Economic Growth*, Vol. 1A, edited by Philippe Aghion and Steven N. Durlauf. Amsterdam: North-Holland.

Acemoglu, D., S. Naidu, P. Restrepo, and J. Robinson. 2019. "Democracy Does Cause Growth." *Journal of Political Economy* 127 (1): 47–100.

Acemoglu, D., and J. Robinson. 2012. *Why Nations Fail: The Origins of Power, Prosperity and Poverty*. London: Profile Books.

Ahmad, A., and I. Irwin. 2019. "Somalia Case Study." Unpublished, World Bank, Washington, DC.

Chatterjee, P. 2004. *The Politics of the Governed: Reflections on Popular Politics in Most of the World*. New York: Columbia University Press.

Cloutier, M. 2021. "Social Contracts in Sub-Saharan Africa: Concepts and Measurements." Policy Research Working Paper Series, World Bank, Washington, DC.

DfID (Department for International Development). 2010. *The Politics of Poverty: Elites, Citizens and States: Findings from Ten Years of DfID-Funded Research on Governance and Fragile States, 2001–2010*. London: DfID. http://www.dfid.gov.uk/Documents /publications1/evaluation/plcy-pltcs-dfid-rsch-synth-ppr.pdf.

Easterly, W., J. Ritzen, and M. Woolcock. 2006. "Social Cohesion, Institutions and Growth." *Economics and Politics* 18 (2): 103–20.

Fukuyama, F. 1995. *Trust: The Social Virtues and the Creation of Prosperity*. New York: Free Press.

Guiso, L., P. Sapienza, and L. Zingales. 2016. "Long-Term Persistence." *Journal of the European Economic Association* 14 (6): 1401–36.

Hanson, J. K., and R. Sigman. 2013. "Leviathan's Latent Dimensions: Measuring State Capacity for Comparative Political Research." American Political Science Association 2011 Annual Meeting Paper.

Hoogeveen, J. 2018. "A Social Contract Indicator for Sub-Sahara Africa." Unpublished, World Bank, Washington, DC.

Howard, P. N., A. Duffy, D. Freelon, M. M. Hussain, W. Mari, and M. Maziad. 2011. "Opening Closed Regimes: What Was the Role of Social Media during the Arab Spring?" Project on Information Technology and Political Islam, University of Washington, Seattle.

Khan, M. 2010. "Political Settlements and the Governance of Growth-Enhancing Institutions." Working Paper, School of Oriental and African Studies, University of London. http://eprints.soas.ac.uk/9968/.

OECD (Organisation for Economic Co-operation and Development). 2009. "Concepts and Dilemmas of State-Building in Fragile Situations: From Fragility to Resilience." *OECD Journal on Development* 9 (3): 61–148.

Putnam, R. 2000. *Bowling Alone: The Collapse and Revival of American Community*. New York: Simon and Schuster.

Putnam, R., R. Leonardis, and R. Nanetti. 1993. *Making Democracy Work: Civic Traditions in Modern Italy*. Princeton: Princeton University Press.

Rasul, I., and D. Rogger. 2016. "Management of Bureaucrats and Public Service Delivery: Evidence from the Nigerian Civil Service." *Economic Journal* 128 (608): 413–46 .

Slater, D. 2011. *Ordering Power: Contentious Politics and Authoritarian Leviathans in Southeast Asia*. Cambridge, U.K.: Cambridge University Press.

Story, W. 2013. "Social Capital and Health in the Least Developed Countries: A Critical Review of the Literature and Implications for a Future Research Agenda." *Global Public Health* 8 (9): 983–99.

Tidjani Alou, M. 2019. "L'Etat et les contrats sociaux au Niger: Eléments d'approche." Unpublished, World Bank, Washington, DC.

van Rijn, F., E. Bulte, and A. Adekunle. 2012. "Social Capital and Agricultural Innovation in Sub-Saharan Africa." *Agricultural Systems* 108: 112–22.

Watts, M. 2019. "States, Societies and Citizenship: The Changing Social Contract in Post-Apartheid South Africa." Unpublished, University of California, Berkeley.

World Bank. 2017. *World Development Report 2017: Governance and the Law*. Washington, DC: World Bank.

Chapter 4

Application: Country Case Studies

The Conceptual Framework in Context

Some common features, albeit manifested in different ways, characterize the nature of social contracts across Africa. This report does not suggest a common social contract narrative for the region. Instead, it unpacks the concept to allow for its application to different contexts. At the same time, as evidenced in the existing literature and the program's case studies, a number of common characteristics of development in the region are fundamental to understanding the often-skewed bargaining dynamics between citizens and the state.

The first of the common features is the historical legacy of colonialism and state formation. In most cases, social contracts in Africa have enabled the building of nation-states where they did not previously exist and in challenging circumstances, but often in ways that rely on elite bargains and forms of rent and patronage that compromise the public interest. These social contracts have taken different forms since independence, including centralized "developmental patrimonialism," military coercion, and "competitive clientelism." In certain circumstances, relatively stable settlements increasingly constrained by decreasing resources have fragmented (as in Côte d'Ivoire in the early 2000s). Conversely, the 2010 decade has seen elite settlements founded upon military-liberation struggles translate into relatively stable pacts that have begun to deliver positive development outcomes (for example, Ethiopia and Rwanda). In a number of instances, elite bargains have not held together, or regions have been left with limited statehood, leading to fragmentation or violence (hence, the large number of states in Africa that appear on the harmonized Fragility, Conflict, and Violence list). All of the case studies carried out under this task illustrate the role of elite bargains in maintaining stability (or failing to do so) and the costs such bargains have imposed on the space for citizen-state bargaining.

Second, citizen-state relations are heavily mediated by other actors and interests. Perhaps unique to Africa is the indirect relationship between the state and much of the citizenry. Much has been said about the evolution and role of traditional or customary authority in Africa (for example, Mamdani 1996), but these features are widely heterogeneous across the continent. In some cases, traditional or religious authorities are formally or explicitly integrated as intermediaries; in others they exercise de facto control over public goods (see the Senegal case study later in this chapter regarding the role of Sufi orders). The interests of these authorities can be aligned in ways that sometimes promote public goods, such as the role of chiefs in delivering public goods in Zambia (Baldwin 2015), or in ways that compete with and undermine citizen-state relationships.[1] Importantly, at the community level, local social contracts can be significant sources of public goods and resilience, including through informal social protection arrangements.[2] Although such arrangements can be important supplements or even de facto substitutes for the state, they are limited and increasingly coming under pressure from demographic and social change.

Third, electoral politics favors short time horizons and clientelist behavior. Poorly institutionalized programmatic political parties combined with relatively low levels of education and high levels of communal identity means political survival often depends on appealing to identity issues and short-term visible goods (like private handouts) while maintaining patrimonial networks through rents (Fujiwara and Wantchekon 2013; Mkandawire 2015). Ample evidence indicates that such clientelist behavior results in lower provision of public services (Habyarimana et al. 2007; Khemani 2015; World Bank 2017), which, in turn, generates a negative feedback loop, in which low and nondevelopmental expectations (subsidies, unrealized promises of free services) are cemented (Resnick 2010). Some research has demonstrated that efforts to increase voter information about candidates can loosen ethnic and party loyalty, and that when electoral competition is more intense, politicians respond with increased provision of local public goods.[3]

Fourth, the demographics of a largely dispersed rural population (often excluded from the market), a small middle class, and a limited independent private sector constrain collective action and shape citizen expectations from the state. A dispersed, subsistence rural population is easy to control through appeals to identity and handouts. Although there is much hope about the emergent middle class in Africa, the literature points to limited impact for social contract bargaining, in part because of the middle class's tendency to either be linked to the political class or to have the means of opting out of public services. Similarly, without a sufficiently diversified and independent private sector, there is little pressure to break out of the dynamics of capture and cronyism (Resnick 2015).

Fifth, natural resource dependence contributes to undermining citizen-state accountability. Much has been written about the "resource curse" and the impact that windfalls from resource rents have on citizen-state accountability. Nigeria, as the case study in this chapter shows, is a prime example of a social contract that has been shaped by the interaction of state-controlled oil resources with a large, complex, multireligious, and multi-ethnic society. On the one hand, oil rents have enabled some level of stability in an extremely fractured environment through fiscal federalism. On the other, they have cemented a system of elite payoffs and corruption with growing inequality that undermines both sound macro-fiscal management and investment in public goods (Usman 2018; Watts 2018a).

Sixth, aid dependence and other transnational factors can undermine social contracts. An ample literature argues that aid can undermine citizen bargaining dynamics with the state (de Waal 2017) through several channels, including by making states accountable to donor priorities, which may differ from citizens' priorities, and by undercutting tax-bargaining dynamics by providing windfall resources (see Prichard 2015; World Bank 2017, chapter 9). Various dimensions of globalization—from structural adjustment policies, to investments by multinational corporations, to illicit financial flows—constrain the state capability dimension of social contract bargaining (Watts 2018b). The Somalia case study in this chapter highlights the transnational influence on the social contract, arguing that the bargain between the international community and the official central government results in both dependency and detachment from the citizenry.

Importantly, social contracts are not static, but are instead dynamic and fluid and constantly renegotiated at different levels. The case studies point to a number of drivers of change:

- *Constitutional moments.* Independence, introduction of democracy, regime change, and postconflict rebuilding are all critical opportunities for explicit and public renegotiation of the social contract. This was clearly the case in the transition in South Africa and the 1996 constitution (see the South Africa case study in this chapter). In Somalia, the reshaping of the state through a federal model is an opportunity to strengthen the social contract by addressing its multiple layers, including the state–strong man relationships that mediate citizen-state relations. Sudan's post-2019 revolution transitional government has also emphasized the need to rebuild a social contract as a fundamental part of its democratic transition.

- *Structural changes.* Both sudden shifts (for example, natural resource discoveries, fiscal shocks, transnational factors) and the accumulation of gradual demographic changes and technological advances can change incentives and relative power in ways that can alter social contracts. Urbanization, for example, can strengthen collective action, as can digital technologies, but these are not panaceas. Efforts to strengthen state capacity and responsiveness to these pressures can be important to mitigating instability and repressive tendencies.

- *Elite bargains.* The nature of elite bargains is also not static, shifting as political maneuvering and competition change the nature of rent distribution or "pacting" arrangements. The Senegal and South Africa case studies in this chapter show how changes within elite coalitions can open up some areas for more progressive social contracts, while closing off others.

- *Subnational social contracts.* Even if a country-level social contract might be stagnant, there can be significant subnational variation and opportunities for change. A good example is Lagos, Nigeria, where, beginning in 1999, two successive governors were able to put together a reform coalition to renegotiate the social contract by producing significant improvements in transportation and sanitation, which also resulted in increased tax compliance and therefore revenue generation. As members of opposition parties facing hostility from the center, their political survival depended on delivering on popular demands.

- *Sectoral or policy-level opportunities.* Certain policy areas will have their own social contract dynamics and may be amenable to renegotiation. These sector-specific social contracts can, in turn, influence other aspects of the broader social contract.

The study commissioned country experts to undertake analyses of the evolution of the social contract in six countries: Cameroon, Niger, Nigeria, Senegal, Somalia, and South Africa. These case studies illustrate different aspects of the social contract, and also highlight the path-dependency of prevailing contracts, but also moments of change and reform. Outlined below are summaries of the country studies and how they relate to the social contract framework.

Cameroon: Lack of Responsiveness in the Social Contract

Understanding the multifaceted challenges in Cameroon (Fisiy 2019) requires considering many of the structural features that are common to the social contract in Africa. These features include Cameroon's colonial history, the linguistic bifurcation of the country, and the incomplete unification following independence in 1972 that allowed separation aspirations to linger. Other features that have shaped the current social contract in Cameroon and the pressures upon it include an economy heavily dependent on extractives and the rise of a small, urban middle class that has been tied to the public sector. Figures 3.2–3.4 indicate that Cameroon's social contract features characteristics associated with low civil capacity, low inclusiveness, and low resiliency (below median openness and alignment). The country case study paper (Fisiy 2019) addresses many of these aspects, a few of which are summarized here.

The contested and fragile bargain between the state and Cameroon's citizens has revealed a low-inclusiveness social contract that has been stretched, allowing for religious, linguistic, and generational differences to be instrumentalized in the anglo versus francophone Cameroonian crisis. Given Cameroon's historical evolution, the primary emphasis since independence and reunification has been on state-building efforts without equal attention to citizens' rights and duties in a multi-ethnic society. A burgeoning civil society sector, especially faith-based groups and cultural organizations, has, in many instances, become associated with service delivery rather than establishing an accountability mechanism to improve the state's quality of services and inclusiveness. In turn, seeing the state functioning for private gain has increasingly become the norm (Bayart, Ellis, and Hibou 2009; Hibou 2004; Mbembe 2001; Watts 2018b). The mindset of *la politique du ventre*[4] (Bayart 1979) has led to the politics of cooptation based on the logic that *la bouche qui mange ne parle pas.*[5] The privatization of public services has progressively been striking at the very core of the concept of social contract. Furthermore, the state relies "mostly on a few large formal firms for tax revenue, as well as import/export taxes mostly from timber and the oil sector" (World Bank 2016, 76). The state has little need to be responsive to citizens' needs, and the virtuous circle of state-building is not triggered.

Endemic corruption and weak accountability. With growing despondency over the state's inability to deliver on the bargains that constitute the social contract, citizens no longer believe in a dream of shared wealth and prosperity; rather, the acquisition of wealth depends on luck—geography is still destiny—and political connections. Without taxation, citizens get treated as "subjects," beneficiaries of government largess with no voice to hold those who govern them accountable.

State structure and responsiveness to citizens' demands. After 11 years of reunification, Cameroon became a unitary state through the 1972 referendum, which put an end to the federalist system, based mainly on the economic argument that the cost of running the two-state federalist system of government was expensive. When the Anglophone crisis erupted in 2016, the federalist agitators, who used the protests initially organized by lawyers and teachers to fight for their sectoral rights, boisterously advocated that the country should revert to the pre-1972 two-state federal structure. These separatists used the metaphor of a failed marriage, arguing that the logical next step should be divorce.

Niger: Basis for a Responsive Social Contract

Niger is at the heart of a turbulent region marked by political and religious violence in northern Nigeria, armed movements in central Mali, and intercommunal violence and state collapse in southern Libya. According to the case study (Tidjani Alou 2019), following independence, Niger experienced 30 years of authoritarian regimes, and the only relations with citizens were based on subordination or confrontation. This phase was followed by a tumultuous transition period between 1992 and 2011, with multiple coups. The 2011 democratic transition was accompanied by a participative public debate on a new constitution, which attracted a lot of public attention on topics such as the duration of electoral mandates, the level of education of elected officials, and the role of the state. These debates involved many social organizations such as unions and associations that regularly use both traditional means like protests and strikes and modern ones such as social media. These organizations have been major actors in the democratization of Niger and were in the front row during the National Conference of 1991, the citizen mobilization on the cost of life—*la vie chère*—of 2005, and the protests around fiscal measures in 2018 and 2019. The kind of civic bargaining underlined in the social contract framework, as well as political and social dialogue such as the sanction of power through elections, is a part of governance that is still new, and society is acclimating to it very slowly.

The case study's observations on Niger's social contract are consistent with the empirical typologies. Niger is a country with significant civil capacity given its level of state capacity. The case study also emphasizes the role of democracy (both in its electoral and associative forms), a major bargaining mechanism of the social contract, and the public debates around the constitutional reforms suggest that the openness of the state represents its resilience. According to the empirical measurements, Niger exhibits a relatively highly resilient social contract compared with other countries in the region, which could be connected to why Niger is faring better than some of its neighbors that have been experiencing social unrest and conflict since the mid-2010s.

Nigeria: Challenges for the Social Contract in Oil-Rich Contexts

Strengthening the social contract has been identified as a necessary condition for Nigeria to achieve greater and shared prosperity (World Bank 2019). The challenge of postcolonial nation-building in Nigeria was to build a robust and inclusive social contract out of a deeply regionalized and sectarian, multi-ethnic, multireligious polity in which oil revenues are central. The demands of constructing an inclusive social contract increased as the country fell into civil war between 1967 and 1970. Nigeria is characterized by a durable political settlement underpinned by oil and managed through fiscal federalism. Although it is a diverse pluri-ethnic society, the centralized accumulation of oil resources risks shifting the balance of power in favor of a single group; Nigeria manages this risk primarily through an extensive institutional federal apparatus that aims to ensure that all groups have protected access to public resources.

The indicators in chapter 3 point to several salient aspects of the social contract in Nigeria: questions of state legitimacy, compromised state capacity, limited social inclusiveness, and low state (and civil) capacity. However, these indicators necessarily paint an aggregate picture and miss the forces that produce the particular shape of the social contract. A complex federal system such as that of Nigeria embodies much heterogeneity in capacity, effectiveness, and responsiveness across sectors and ministries, between states within the federation, and even at the level of city and local government. Hence, the question of civil capacity requires careful consideration in Nigeria. The lack of citizen cooperation reflects political and electoral violence, competitive struggles over the allocation of access to oil revenues and rents, and the existence since about 2009 of two major insurgencies.

The case study (Watts 2019) argues that postcolonial Nigeria has constructed a social contract in and through the state capture of oil rents, which has produced an "elite cartel" at the center of the social contract. Nigeria's social contract has been shaped by the interaction of state-controlled oil resources with a large, complex, multireligious and multi-ethnic society. Since the oil boom in the 1970s, oil revenues reoriented an already-fractious social contract around rent distribution via a multi-ethnic provisioning pact. Beginning in 1999, a multiparty democracy produced an unstable, exclusionary, and turbulent social contract held together by an elite consensus around power and rent distribution. Protest movements and violence are some of the mechanisms through which excluded groups attempt to contest this distribution of resources.

Over time, Nigeria has developed a set of formal and informal institutions by which the social contract links the state and citizens, designed to produce the consent of and legitimacy among contending ethnoregional constituencies. These institutions have comprised (1) *fiscal federalism*: the formal distribution of oil revenues among the federal, state, and local governments; (2) a *federal character*: equitable representation of all of Nigeria's 36 states in the federal cabinet, the army, and the public sector; (3) *political zoning*: grouping of the 36 states into six geopolitical regions; (4) *presidential rotation*: an informal consensus to rotate presidential power every eight years between the North and the South; and (5) *petroleum subsidies*: the distribution of oil proceeds to citizens in the absence of comprehensive social welfare and public goods (education, health, social protection, infrastructure).

Senegal: Collaboration across Actors for a Stable Social Contract

Senegal is the only country in continental West Africa that has never experienced a coup d'état and it has enjoyed expanding democratic freedoms since the reintroduction of multiparty democracy in 1976. Domestically, the traditional form of Sufi Islam has "provided for a substantial social stability, strong cultural identity and laid the foundations for inter-confessional and inter-ethnical harmony" (World Bank 2018b, 9). The case study (Konte 2019) examines this sustained stability by using the social contract lens to analyze four issues that are particularly relevant for Senegal: (1) the role of Sufi modernism in the plurality of the social contract, (2) citizen participation and engagement, (3) inequality and the inclusion of the youth, and (4) the Islamo-Wolof model of the social contract.

The case study observes that the social contract functions as a system for the exchange of services in which the state and Sufi orders, even though apparently situated in different sociopolitical spaces, collaborate in preserving peace and stability. The success of this system largely rests on the capacity of the brotherhoods' leaders to maintain their credibility in the eyes of the population by keeping their distance from those in power to play the role of spokespersons for the voiceless and function as safety valves in times of crisis. The Muridiyya[6] is considered the most important cog in the social contract machine. Support of the Murid sheikhs, regarded as the sole truly legitimate leaders by a sizable segment of the population, is indispensable to ensuring civil peace and the implementation of government projects, particularly the unpopular ones. The status of the Murid sheikhs also connects to the Islamo-Wolof model, which is composed of the political, social, and cultural arrangements (infrastructure and ideologies) that have been both supporting the operations of the colonial and the postcolonial states and providing the sources and resources for the legitimacy of their power. The Islamo-Wolof model binds the state and the brotherhoods in a complex web of social, cultural, economic, and political relationships. It covers the whole social field and, moreover, guarantees the hegemony of a modernity that is Wolof-inspired and driven, both at the ideological level and at the social level in the public sphere. Regarding the civil capacity side of the social contract, the case study observes that citizens in Senegal do not face many constraints to political participation, but the centralization of power in the executive branch at the expense of the legislative and judiciary branches and of local governments makes genuine political participation less meaningful. Senegal's democracy has allowed many centers of influence to emerge and exercise veto power in a highly politicized environment, creating a system good at designing abstract policies, but marked by evident inertia in implementation.

This qualitative analysis contextualizes and complements many of the results highlighted in the empirical framework. The high openness and above-average apparent alignment of the social contract are consistent with the description of political stability and strength of the participatory networks of the Islamo-Wolof model. Similarly, Senegal is comfortably situated in the northeast quadrants of both the capacity and social outcomes typologies (figures 3.2 and 3.3), indicating a social contract characterized by high state and civil capacity as well as provision of public goods and services in a fair manner relative to other countries in the region. The disaggregated empirical framework suggests that there is some underperformance in core areas such as social security, social protection, and education. Low enrollment, low completion, and high repetition rates in the formal education system result in Senegal's adult and youth literacy rates being the lowest across comparator countries. This mirrors the case study's discussion of the fact that large segments of the youth continue to remain outside of mainstream economic and social life, which has led to high youth mobilization and acts of civil disobedience, notably through the critique emanating from Senegal's hip-hop culture, in particular from the opposition group Y'en a Marre.[7]

Somalia: The Role of Nonstate Actors in Shaping the Social Contract

Since the collapse of its central government in 1991, Somalia has been a classic case of state fragility. The crisis not only produced repetitive humanitarian disasters inside the shattered country, but also spilled over into neighboring states, threatening border security and regional stability across the Horn of Africa. Given these extreme consequences, over the past three decades the international community has invested enormous resources in an attempt to rebuild a coherent and responsive Somali state. However, after countless failed and fledgling peace processes, the path to successful state reformation in Somalia remains elusive. Because of data limitations for Somalia, the country appears on only one of the three compasses in chapter 3. On the resilience compass, the indicators suggest that Somalia has among the least-resilient social contracts in the region because of low alignment and low openness.

The case study (Ahmad 2019) posits a conceptual model of the social contract that comprises the three essential bargains that shape and define the political and security landscape in Somalia: (1) the bargain between international partners and the federal government, which results in both dependency and detachment from the citizenry; (2) the negotiated two-level bargain between the central government and local strongmen, which intervenes in the relationship between the state and the citizenry; and (3) the coercive relationship between the violent insurgent group al-Shabaab and the citizenry, which exists parallel to the deals struck with the government and local strongmen.

Most alarmingly, while the official government struggles to establish a direct protection-taxation relationship with its citizens, al-Shabaab has successfully developed its own coercive deal. Across large swaths of the countryside, the insurgency has developed strategies to directly tax citizens across clan lines and to enforce their rule over these populations. Although their methods are extraordinarily abusive, the fact remains that these insurgents have forged a type of protection-taxation relationship that resembles a rudimentary social contract between citizen and state. While the official government has been unable to forge a direct deal with its citizens, al-Shabaab has learned how to effectively tax and govern local populations.

Why then has al-Shabaab had greater success in establishing direct protection and taxation across clan lines while the Somali government has not been able to provide a viable social contract with its citizens? An examination of the fragmentation of the social contract and an effort to model bargains as multiple and competing protection-extortion rackets show that these deals have created perverse incentives that encourage powerholders to behave in ways that undermine true state consolidation. International support for the Somali state has inadvertently encouraged these perverse processes and thus made it more difficult to create a normal social contract between state and citizen.

South Africa: A Dynamic Social Contract

South Africa's political transition is arguably one of the most remarkable in history, but its evolution to an inclusive, prosperous society is still in process (World Bank 2018a). The fragility of the social contract is seen as a symptom of an "incomplete transition." When many citizens are excluded from job opportunities and, hence, from joining the middle class, significant pressure is put on the social contract.

The case study (Watts 2018b) starts with understanding apartheid as a form of social contract predicated on an institutionalized form of racial exclusion, oppression, and inequality. Over the course of the twentieth century, the components of that contract were renegotiated around class and ethnic tensions within the white population as well as the changing strategies of coercion and consent with respect to the black and "colored" populations. The collapse of this codified system of institutionalized racial segregation in the early 1990s produced a negotiated transition of the social contract based on pact-making, bargaining, and brokerage institutions.

The postapartheid social contract was a form of developmental welfarism that started during the Nelson Mandela presidency (1994–1999), though its specific institutional form took shape during the Thabo Mbeki era (1999–2008). It was organized around three policy platforms: (1) massive expansion of the social protection system, focusing principally on mothers and the aged; (2) a strong focus on "deracializing" control of the economy through affirmative action policies designed to fast-track the placement of black people into management and senior management positions; and (3) the transformation of white ownership of the economy through Black Economic Empowerment policies. Mbeki attempted to renegotiate the social contract through an organizational shift of political control away from the African National Congress itself to the presidency, an institution that he sought to build into a powerful apparatus of control and coordination at the center of the state. This shift was resented, particularly by provincial party bosses and black business classes, and the party reestablished control of the state by recalling a sitting state president.

The ascension of Jacob Zuma in 1999 marked a radical unraveling of a nascent democratic contract, displacing the African National Congress as the primary force for transformation in society. The democratic social contract was "repurposed" and replaced by a party hegemony operating like a shadow state, a well-organized network that strives to manage what is often referred to as the symbiotic relationship between the constitutional state and the shadow state. At the center of this repurposed social contract stands a plethora of "broker networks" linking the party elites, controllers, entrepreneurs, brokers, and middlemen, often transnational in scope and cutting across party, business, and ethnic lines.

The indicators developed for this report paint a complex picture of the social contract but one largely consistent with the sense of deepening corruption, state illegitimacy, and civil society activism. South Africa scores slightly above average for civil capacity but also higher for state capacity compared with other African states. The relatively high score for state capacity is driven by high state authority and state effectiveness compared with the other countries in the region, capturing bureaucratic capabilities and patterns of administrative and organizational performance. State capacity does properly reflect, however, the institutional inheritances from the apartheid state and the extensive state-building undertaken since 1994. Civil society capacity is, as expected, quite high, consistent with both the recent history of citizen pressure and engagement and the proliferation of civil society groups and organizations.

When social divides are large, as in South Africa, it is difficult to build a strong social contract. The lack of job opportunities, especially for young people, is putting pressure on the social contract. This pressure is observable in the 2015 protests for free higher education. The *#FeesMustFall* demonstrations beginning in 2015 were partly in response to awareness among young people that tertiary education, which has been unaffordable for many, is critical for obtaining a job. The inequality of income and assets results in contestation for these resources, be it to redress injustices of the past, provide dignity to the most vulnerable, or strengthen the sense of fairness in society. The unequal distribution of resources can also result in illegal and violent forms of contestation, such as crime and corruption (World Bank 2018a).

Notes

1. See Conteh (2017) on decentralization in Sierra Leone and Wilfahrt (2018) on Senegal.
2. See Wantchekon (2003) on Benin and the Somalia case study in this chapter.
3. Casey's (2015) findings are in line with Khemani (2015).
4. The "politics of the belly" refers to politics based on the distribution of food and cash to appease social unrest.
5. A phrase commonly used in Francophone West Africa; it means "the mouth that eats does not speak" and depicts a classic situation of elite cooptation.
6. The Mouride brotherhood is a large tariqa (Sufi order) most prominent in Senegal and The Gambia with headquarters in the city of Touba, Senegal, which is a holy city for the order.
7. Y'en a Marre, or "We are fed up," is a group of Senegalese rappers and journalists, created in January 2011, to protest ineffective government and register youth to vote, and is associated with voting out President Abdoulaye Wade in 2012.

References

Ahmad, A. 2019. "Somalia Case Study." Unpublished, World Bank, Washington, DC.

Baldwin, K. 2015. *The Paradox of Traditional Chiefs in Democratic Africa*. Cambridge, U.K.: Cambridge University Press.

Bayart, J. F. 1979. *L'Etat au Cameroun*, Paris, Foundation Nationale de Sciences Politiques.

Bayart, J. F., S. Ellis, and B. Hibou. 2009. *Criminalizing the State in Africa*. Bloomington, IN: Indiana University Press.

Casey, K. 2015. "Crossing Party Lines: The Effects of Information on Redistributive Politics." *American Economic Review* 105 (8): 2410–48.

Conteh, F. M. 2017. "Politics, Development and the Instrumentalization of (De) Centralization in Sierra Leone." *Review of African Political Economy* 44 (151).

De Waal, A. 2017. *Mass Starvation: The History and Future of Famine*. Cambridge, U.K., Malden, MA: Polity Press.

Fisiy, C. 2019. "Cameroon Case Study." Unpublished, World Bank, Washington, DC.

Fujiwara, T., and L. Wantchekon. 2013. "Can Informed Public Deliberation Overcome Clientelism? Experimental Evidence from Benin." *American Economic Journal: Applied Economics* 5 (4): 241–55.

Habyarimana, J., M. Humphreys, D. N. Posner, and J. M. Weinstein. 2007. "Why Does Ethnic Diversity Undermine Public Goods Provision?" *American Political Science Review* 101 (4): 709–25.

Hibou, B. 2004. *Privatizing the State.* New York: Columbia University Press.

Khemani, S. 2015. "Buying Votes versus Supplying Public Services: Political Incentives to Under-Invest in Pro-Poor Policies." *Journal of Development Economics* 177 (C): 84–93.

Konte, M. 2019. "Senegal Case Study." Unpublished, World Bank, Washington, DC.

Mamdani, M. 1996. *Citizen and Subject: Contemporary Africa and the Legacy of Late Colonialism.* Princeton: Princeton University Press.

Mbembe, A. 2001. *On the Postcolony.* Berkeley, CA: University of California Press.

Mkandawire, Thandika. 2015. "Neopatrimonialism and the Political Economy of Economic Performance in Africa: Critical Reflections." *World Politics* 67 (3): 563–612.

Prichard, W. 2015. *Taxation, Responsiveness and Accountability in Sub-Saharan Africa: The Dynamics of Tax Bargaining.* Cambridge, U.K.: Cambridge University Press.

Resnick, D. 2010. "Populist Strategies in Africa." UNU-WIDER Working Paper 2010/114, United Nations University–World Institute for Development Economics Research, Helsinki.

Resnick, D. 2015. "The Political Economy of Africa's Emergent Middle Class: Retrospect and Prospects." *Journal of International Development* 27 (5): 573–87.

Tidjani Alou, M. 2019. "Niger Case Study." Unpublished, World Bank, Washington, DC.

Usman, Z. 2018. "The 'Resource Curse' and Constraints to Reforming Nigeria's Oil Sector." In *The Oxford Handbook of Nigerian Politics*, edited by C. Levan and P. Ukata, 520–44. Oxford: Oxford University Press.

Wantchekon, L. 2003. "Clientelism and Voting Behavior." *World Politics* 55 (April): 399–422.

Watts, M. 2018a. "Political Settlements in Nigeria." Unpublished, University of California, Berkeley.

Watts, M. 2018b. "States, Societies and Social Contracts: Understanding State Capacity, Political Orders and Civic Society Engagement in Africa." Unpublished, University of California, Berkeley.

Watts, M. 2019. "*Nigeria Case Study.*" Unpublished, World Bank, Washington, DC.

Wilfahrt, M. 2018. "The Politics of Local Government Performance: Elite Cohesion and Cross-Village Constraints in Decentralized Senegal." *World Development* 103: 149–61.

World Bank. 2016. "Republic of Cameroon—Priorities for Ending Poverty & Boosting Shared Prosperity: Systematic Country Diagnostic." Report 103098-CM, World Bank Group, Washington, DC.

World Bank. 2017. *World Development Report 2017: Governance and the Law.* Washington, DC: World Bank.

World Bank. 2018a. "An Incomplete Transition: Overcoming the Legacy of Exclusion in South Africa. South Africa Systematic Country Diagnostic." World Bank, Washington, DC.

World Bank. 2018b. "Systematic Country Diagnostic of Senegal." World Bank, Washington, DC.

World Bank. 2019. "Nigeria on the Move: A Journey to Inclusive Growth. Systematic Country Diagnostic." World Bank, Washington, DC.

Chapter 5

Application: Sectoral and Thematic Spotlights

The study underlying this report examined how social contract dynamics shape and are shaped by a number of sectors and themes. The first spotlight explores how social protection is increasingly shaping and being shaped by social contracts in Africa. The second spotlight highlights the fiscal contract as a specific component of the broader social contract and how tax compliance, trust, and state capacity are related in a context of often low taxation. The third sectoral spotlight expands on the challenges social contracts face in resource-rich countries. The fourth spotlight highlights the role of fragmented social contracts as a driver of conflict, and how conflict prevention and peacebuilding can benefit from a social contract framing. The fifth spotlight describes recent protest trends in Africa and highlights their roles as social contract negotiation events. The sixth spotlight introduces a normative role for social contracts within the context of human rights. The seventh spotlight highlights the role of the social contract when designing and implementing policies aimed at addressing inequality and redistribution. The eighth spotlight examines how social accountability tools can be used to strengthen social contracts. Finally, the ninth spotlight looks at social contracts in the context of the COVID-19 (coronavirus) pandemic that began in 2020.

Social Protection: Increasingly Shaping and Being Shaped by Social Contracts in Africa

Social protection programs encapsulate the expectation (and attendant obligation) that states will provide a basic level of protection to society's most vulnerable.

Emerging from social contract ideas that states and citizens have rights and responsibilities toward one other, social protection programs rest on citizens' delegation of authority to the state. Citizen consent, in turn, stems from the government's commitment to protect its citizens from harm. Social protection connects to many aspects of the framework presented in this report. It often is a responsibility of the state and therefore the way it is implemented affects the thickness and inclusiveness of social contracts.

Africa has seen a significant expansion of social protection programs over the past two decades (figure 5.1). More than 45 countries now have social safety net programs in place to address chronic poverty and to help poor households diversify their livelihoods and invest in their children's health and education. During COVID-19, many countries began significantly expanding their social protection programs, including social assistance, insurance, and labor market programs (Gentilini et al. 2020). However, owing to fiscal and capacity constraints, and arguably also political economy related to prevailing social contracts, social safety net programs often cover only a small proportion of the poor and are concentrated in rural areas, where chronic poverty is highest (and also where many governments in power find a significant political base) (Beegle et al. 2018).

The rapid expansion of social protection schemes in the region indicates that this type of support is one of the returns that citizens increasingly expect

Figure 5.1 Establishment of Safety Nets in Africa

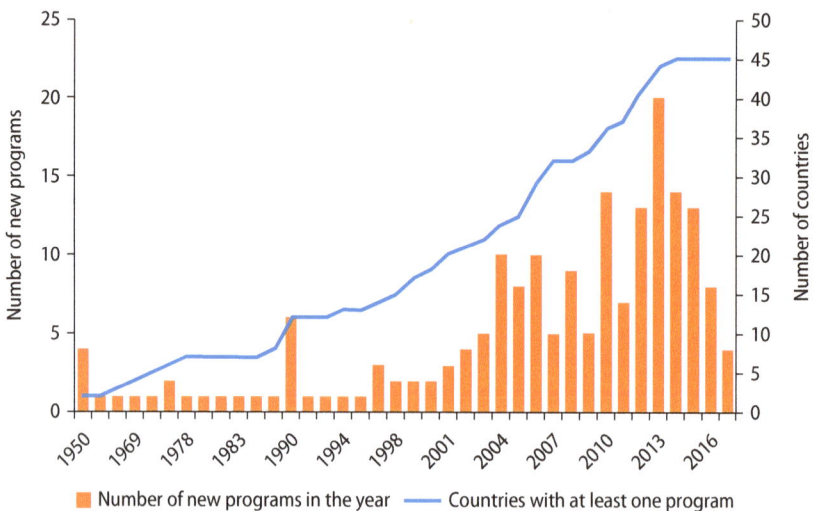

Source: Adapted from Beegle et al. 2018.

from governments in Africa. In fact, social protection is a service that is particularly important at the local level, often being the first or one of the few positive encounters of vulnerable citizens with the central state. As a result, social protection programs can shape citizens' confidence in state institutions and consequent willingness to delegate authority (Sacks 2012). There is, therefore, a two-way relationship between social protection programs and social contracts: the latter are an expression (outcome) of the former, but the former are also a force in the making and remaking (inclusiveness, thickness) of the social contract.

There are four main features of social protection programming through which program design can shape citizen-state relations (based on Dreier, Alik-Lagrange, and Lake [2020] and Dreier et al. [2021]), affecting what governments provide to citizens as well as citizens' delegation and consent to be governed (Levi and Stoker 2000; Risse and Stollenwerk 2018). These four features of social protection program design are formalization, the degree of state partnership, conditionality, and targeting that shapes the nature of state-society relations.

The first set of features, formalization, can affect state capacity. Many social protection programs in Africa are being expanded and upgraded with the help of social registries and technology (for administration but also, for example, for payments) (Lindert et al. 2020). Creating citizen registries and introducing technological innovations can bolster state capacity, infrastructure, and surveillance. Even without extensive state involvement, social protection programs can serve to consolidate and centralize the exercise of state power. These effects can be economically expedient and politically stabilizing. However, in states with enduring legacies of violence and oppression, social protection programming that increases states' monitoring and surveillance capabilities can also be harnessed for more politically sinister authoritarian agendas (Beresford, Berry, and Mann 2018).

The second set of features, the degree of state partnership, affects civil capacity. Poverty reduction and the alleviation of associated harms can enhance individual and community participation in social, political, and economic life (Carpenter, Mallett, and Slater 2012). Increased public participation and engagement in these realms can reconstitute individuals as citizens with rights, responsibilities, and duties that derive from their membership in a broader polity and extend beyond their immediate communities and kinship networks.

The third and fourth features of social protection programs can shape social contract outcomes more directly through their impact on the thickness, inclusiveness, or legitimacy of the social contract. One of the most fundamental decisions required when designing any social protection program has to do with determining the eligible population and final beneficiaries (that is, targeting). Despite increasing debate about the merits of universal approaches to social protection programs, given limited resources and efficiency considerations, programs are most often targeted through a variety of mechanisms (for example, community based, geographical targeting, categorical targeting, proxy-means testing). Yet, the decision to target, and how to do it, can have significant implications beyond the program itself: Is it considered fair? When are errors of inclusion acceptable to avoid exclusion? Is there a legitimate actor, even if not the state, that can justify the targeting and the mechanism chosen? How do considerations about the social contract enter when making these decisions?

Program conditionality can consolidate state authority, cement the rule of law, and contribute to the building of human capital through investments in health and education, for example. In doing this, conditionalities reflect, but can also impose, a social contract arrangement between citizens and the state. Thus, which conditionalities can strengthen the overall social contract at the local and national level? Which behaviors can generate a virtuous cycle to help communities and countries move to a better equilibrium in their social contract? Are there cases in which conditions can have negative effects on social contract dynamics? Background work commissioned for this report (Dreier, Alik-Lagrange, and Lake 2020) illustrates these patterns with specific programmatic examples, highlighting promising avenues for advancing democratic accountability and citizen participation while guarding against strengthened authoritarian control.

The Taxation Challenge in Africa: Cause and Effect of Prevailing Social Contracts

Many countries in Africa struggle to collect taxes, partly both a cause and a consequence of prevailing social contracts. The collected tax[1] to gross domestic product (GDP) ratio in the region is, on average, 19 percent, but there is wide variation across countries, with taxes equating to less than 1 percent of GDP in Somalia and between 7 and 10 percent in countries such as Angola, Ethiopia, and Madagascar. In contrast, in Namibia and South Africa, taxes equate to about 27–28 percent of GDP.[2] In countries where tax collection is low, the capacity of the state to provide services is undermined, thus possibly undermining the stability of the social contract. Hence, a key challenge for many countries in Africa is to be able to increase taxation and to improve the accompanying use of resources.

The World Bank, through its Innovations in Tax Compliance project, which accounts for social contract dynamics, has developed a conceptual framework for developing more effective approaches to tax reform and compliance in developing countries (Prichard et al. 2019). The project places fiscal contracts squarely at the center of its approach to tax reform. It goes beyond traditional approaches that rely solely on enforcement and facilitation and brings in trust. By combining

complementary investments in enforcement and facilitation with trust, reform-
ers can not only strengthen enforced compliance but also can (1) encourage quasi-voluntary compliance, (2) generate sustainable political support for
reform, and (3) create conditions that are more conducive to the construction
of stronger fiscal contracts. This approach raises the question of what the relation is between taxation, fiscal contracts, and dynamic social contracts as illustrated by figure 3.1 in this report. The tax compliance framework of the fiscal
contract connects to many aspects of the social contract framework proposed in
this report, including the relation between state capacity, tax enforcement, and
revenue mobilization; the importance of the citizen-state bargain in the reform
process; and the fiscal contract as a driver of responsiveness and state accountability, an idea also explored in the spotlight on natural resources.

Taxation is an integral part of many social contracts; it is the result of a
bargaining process between citizens and states. Put in its simplest form, states
seek to raise revenue, and citizens expect to receive services in exchange while
also trying to minimize their tax liabilities. Although states can coerce citizens
into paying, they typically do not have the capacity to coerce taxpayers into full
compliance. Therefore, states have to make concessions to taxpayers to secure
quasi-voluntary compliance. Put differently, citizens will be less reluctant to pay
their taxes if they are satisfied with what they receive in return for their taxes
and if they feel like they have influence over what happens with their taxes.
Taxation thus generates incentives for explicit and implicit "tax bargaining"
between citizens and states, as increased tax collection is exchanged for greater
responsiveness and accountability. In turn, this process may provide the basis
for the construction of durable fiscal contracts (Levi 1988; Moore 2004), which
contribute in important ways to social contract outcomes, strengthening the
overall social contract.

Through its impact on the social contract, taxation contributes to state-
building by possibly bringing about more capable, responsive, and accountable
governments. Research highlights the historical centrality of taxation to state-
building and the expansion of political accountability in early modern Europe
in particular. In their search for revenue to finance wars, states expanded taxation but were also forced to expand accountability to secure the support and tax
compliance of wealthy taxpayers, leading to the emergence of national assem-
blies (Tilly 1990). The availability of alternative sources of finance, such as aid
and natural resource revenues, has cast some doubt on whether this mechanism still works for contemporary developing countries (Moore 2015). This
challenge is particularly salient in a number of African countries, where the
ability to raise tax revenues from other sources is limited, increasing reliance,
when the resources exist, on these other forms of revenue where the stakes for
the population tend to be more obscure, making accountability more difficult.
However, a growing body of literature suggests that taxation still contributes to

the development of more responsive and accountable states (Prichard 2015). Somaliland's dependence on local tax revenue, for example, provided those outside the government with the necessary leverage to press for inclusive, representative, and accountable institutions (Eubank 2012).

The social contract itself also affects taxation because taxpayers' compliance depends on their bargain with the state. Traditionally, approaches to tax compliance have stressed the importance of enforcement and, more recently, of facilitation. This focus has reflected early models of tax compliance, which presented the decision to comply as the product of the cost of the penalty for noncompliance and the cost of compliance (Allingham and Sandmo 1972). However, looked at through the prism of a fiscal contract, tax compliance equally depends on whether citizens trust that they will get something in return for the taxes they pay, that is, that the state will uphold its end of the fiscal contract. Recent research finds that where fairness, equity, reciprocity, and accountability—the different dimensions of trust—feature more prominently, taxpayers are not only more likely to comply but also more willing to support reform (Gatt and Owen 2018).

Challenges for a Responsive Social Contract in Resource-Rich Countries in Africa

The social contract in Africa's resource-rich countries often features distinct bargaining dynamics and tends to be less responsive. In countries endowed with nonrenewable resources, that is, oil, gas, and minerals, the nature of citizen-state relations has identifiable characteristics. There are 19 mineral-rich and 12 oil-rich economies on the continent, defined by the International Monetary Fund as having mineral or oil rents accounting for at least 25 percent of their exports (Lundren, Thomas, and York 2013). In these resource exporters, the institutional mechanisms of accountability are profoundly shaped and, in extreme cases, distorted by resource revenues. Because the state derives most of its revenue from an external source, policy makers can feel less obligated to provide public goods. Citizens can have limited influence on policy makers to effectively demand public services. External factors, including commodity price swings, can be hugely disruptive, reinforcing or providing an opening for renegotiation of the social contract in meaningful or destructive ways. These resource revenues, especially via oil, have a structuring effect on institutions (Ross 2012) through their scale (volume), source (not from taxes), stability (volatility and unpredictability), and secrecy (easily hidden).

However, it is not necessarily the existence or features of these resources that cause social contracts to have these characteristics, but the sociopolitical context of their utilization. Resource-rich countries share certain properties of "stateness" and decision-making unless significant state-building has occurred before a resource windfall (Karl 1997). In other words, citizen-state relations can be profoundly influenced by the timing of a resource windfall—whether it occurs in the early stage of state-building when institutions are still malleable or in the latter stages when institutions have set. Thus, Botswana is one of Africa's most stable and prosperous middle-income countries today partly because when diamond mining began in the 1970s, there was already a strong and stable social contract that built on precolonial institutions and that incorporated the interests of various groups in society on the platform of the Botswana Democratic Party (Sebudubudu and Botlhomilwe 2011). With stable institutions underpinned by an inclusive political coalition, Botswana has prudently managed its diamond revenues; invested substantially in building human, physical, and social capital; and accumulated foreign reserves, including a well-managed sovereign wealth fund (African Natural Resources Center 2016).

A key characteristic of the social contract in resource-rich countries is that policy makers often have limited obligations to provide public goods and social welfare. Policy makers are less constrained to be responsive to society because the state derives most of its revenue from external rather than domestic sources. Therefore, institutional checks and restraints toward accountability, such as executive, legislative, and civil society oversight, are neither strong nor effective. It is not unusual in these countries, especially those that are oil-rich, to derive little value from massive public expenditures. Despite large and prestigious infrastructure projects, such as roads, airports, stadiums, and global tournaments, human capital investments can be lower, and their outcomes often poorer, than in resource-poor countries (figure 5.2). Public investments can easily be squandered by corrupt and unaccountable elites because these resource revenues are easily amenable to diversion. To address this issue, it has been suggested that if, instead of making unaccountable public-spending decisions with their oil revenues, governments were to distribute these revenues directly to citizens (in equal amounts to all citizens), and then tax them to finance public goods, there would be at least two effects. First, citizens would have a better idea of how extensive the revenues are. Second, because expenditures are being financed from their tax payments, citizens may have greater incentive to scrutinize these expenditures (Devarajan 2017).

Another characteristic of the social contract in Africa's resource-rich countries is that citizens have limited avenues through which to influence decision-making. The unique impacts of the Dutch disease in low-income economies at an early stage of development profoundly undermine structural industrial transformation. Producer groups, business associations, and trade unions that would normally be the important institutional mechanisms for influencing public policy tend to be weak because of the low productivity and limited competitiveness in sectors such as agriculture, manufacturing, and other tradables.

Figure 5.2 The World's Poverty Share among Resource-Rich and Nonresource-Rich Countries in Africa

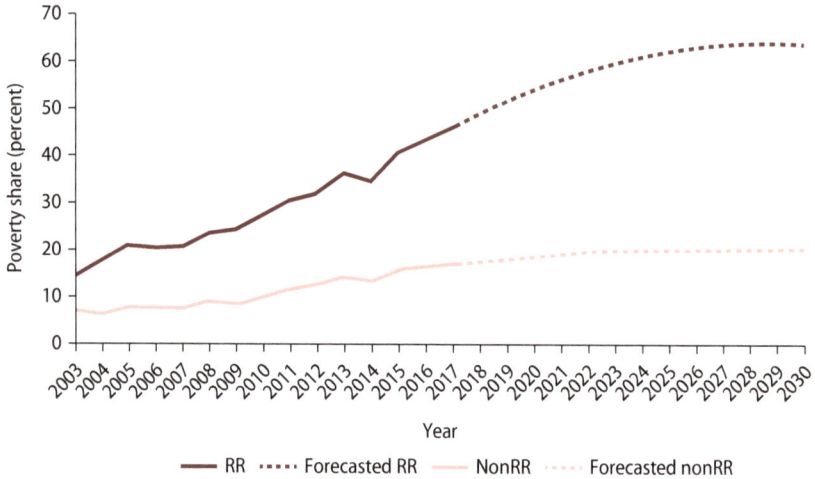

Source: Cust and Zeufack, forthcoming.
Note: RR = resource rich.

Given the weak productivity and competitiveness of these tradables sectors, they generate limited revenues through the mechanisms of export earnings and taxes (figure 5.3). The tax capacity of these countries remains small and under-developed. Within this context, it is not uncommon for decision-making to be captive to special interest groups, such as privileged elites, multinationals, and other large firms operating within and around the resource sector.

Opportunities for renegotiating the social contract occur at critical junctures coinciding with external shocks. Because of resource-rich countries' economic dependence on global commodity markets, these shocks tend to come from sharp global price swings. During periods of high commodity prices, oil and mineral windfalls provide the revenues to sustain and reinforce the status quo; autocratic governments awash with petrodollars coerce and coopt citizens; the Dutch disease results in severe import dependence to the detriment of the pro-ductive sectors; and policy makers are insulated from pressures for account-ability. However, the sudden collapse of global commodity prices, especially in oil-rich countries, creates strong fiscal pressures that can lead to a renewed reform orientation among policy makers (Usman 2020). Such policy reforms include tax, public financial management, and domestic resource mobiliza-tion; a market orientation toward commercialization and privatization of state-owned enterprises; and deregulation and liberalization of key sectors such as

Figure 5.3 Oil-Poor Countries Outperform Oil-Rich Countries in Tax Collection

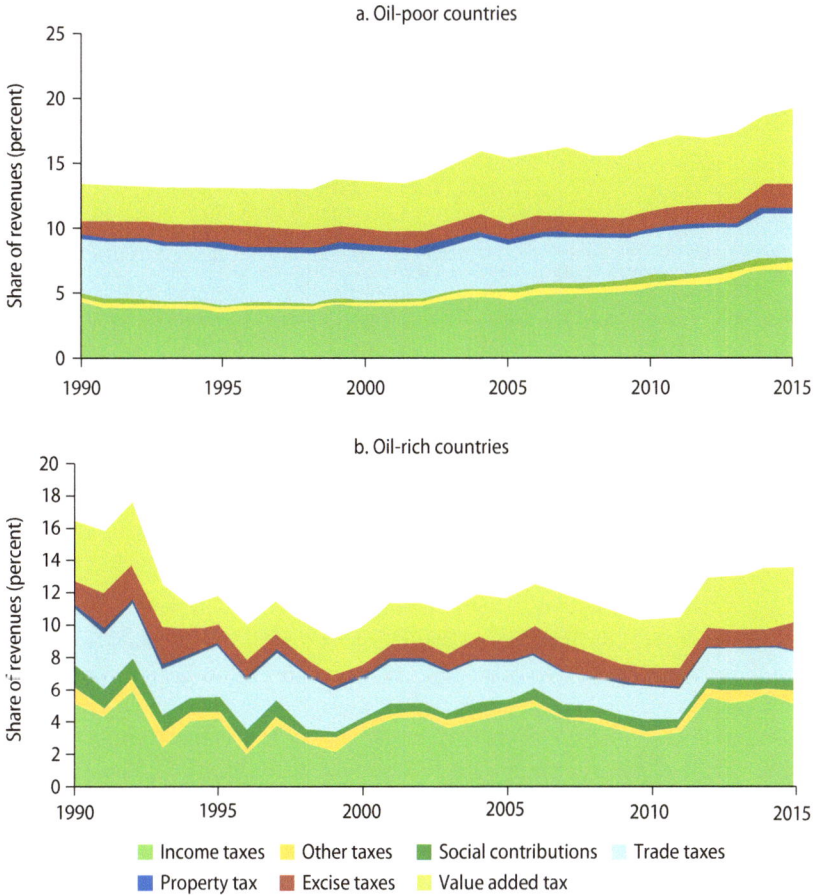

a. Oil-poor countries

b. Oil-rich countries

Income taxes | Other taxes | Social contributions | Trade taxes
Property tax | Excise taxes | Value added tax

Source: Choi, Dutz, and Usman 2020.

energy, trade, and financial services. Reforms that lead to a greater reliance on tax revenues and enable the participation of new and more private actors in the economy can ultimately tilt the balance of power and reorient citizen-state relations.

Other external shocks that may disrupt the social contract in these resource-rich countries include technological change and the energy transition. The digital technologies driving the fourth industrial revolution are set to change the business models and operations of the mining sector in ways that could have profound socioeconomic implications for mineral-rich countries in Africa. A case study of mining companies in a high-income country and a lower-middle income country concludes that as new technologies are rolled out, host countries will be at risk of reduced socioeconomic benefits from mining because of lost local employment and personal income tax revenue, and employment-related local procurement will also suffer (Cosbey et al. 2016). Similarly, the ongoing global transition to clean energy technologies propelled by the 2015 Paris Agreement on Climate Change may depress the long-term global demand for oil and gas from Africa's producers. Mineral exporters are likely to see sharp demand growth for "climate minerals," such as cobalt, copper, iron, lithium, and nickel for use in solar panels, wind turbines, batteries, and other renewable energy hardware (Arrobas et al. 2017). In both cases, disruptions to long-term global demand for oil, gas, and minerals will affect the revenues available to policy makers, the benefits of these resources accruing to citizens and communities, and therefore the balance in citizen-state relations.

The Role of Social Contract Fragmentation in Conflict and Fragility

Of the 30 fragile and conflict-affected situations on the World Bank's Fragility, Conflict, and Violence harmonized list, 18 are in African states, where violence and weak institutional capacity remain major impediments to shared prosperity on the continent. The use of social contract theory in the literature on peacebuilding and conflict is undergoing a resurgence (for example, Kaplan 2014; Leonard 2013; McCandless 2018a). This revival has been partly driven by events such as the Arab Spring (Devarajan and Ianchovichina 2018; Toska 2017), and partly by a reaction to the focus in the discourse on elite bargains (World Bank 2011) and political settlements (Di John and Putzel 2009). The alignment and openness compass presented in the framework relates to conflict and fragility. The assumption is that social unrest can be a response to a low level of alignment between citizens' perceptions of the outcomes of the social contract and their expectations. When this misalignment is combined with a lack of responsiveness from the state, unrest and violence could arise as a last resort form of bargain or as a breakdown in the social contract. The role of unrest as a bargaining mechanism is further described in the next spotlight.

This study finds that the degree to which the state is responsive and a "people-centered approach to [conflict] prevention" (United Nations and World Bank 2019, 277) can be realized is contingent on the nature of the citizen-state bargain. The South Africa case study (Watts 2019) shows the importance of the strength of civil capacity, as epitomized by the mobilization within the African

National Congress, in shaping the social contract that emerged in 1994 and the fall of apartheid.

In examining the nature of violence or the fragility of a peace process, the social contract framework is useful to gaining an understanding of the causes of armed conflict as well as state and civil capacity while countries are in conflict. Furthermore, it can be used to help define the policy and operational options for external institutions in advancing peacebuilding and development objectives.

The theory of the causes of conflict has been dominated by two approaches—greed and grievance (Berdal and Malone 2000). The greed hypothesis posits that the availability of rents and resources provides the interest and opportunity for rebel groups to rise up against the state (Collier and Hoeffler 2004). The grievance hypothesis suggests that armed conflict arises from relative deprivation, horizontal inequality (Stewart 2008), and polarization (Esteban and Schneider 2008), creating drivers for collective action and mobilization of group identity around arenas of contestation (United Nations and World Bank 2019).

However, there may be contexts in which the fault lines of greed and grievance exist, but the social contract is sufficiently resilient to prevent the triggering of armed violence (Murshed 2009). An insufficiently inclusive or responsive social contract can lead to narrow elite bargaining, interrupted transitions of power, and a breakdown of the "rules of the game," resulting in armed violence. Such breakdowns include those of the arrangements around fiscal revenue sharing (for example, Nigeria) and unstable transitions after the death of a head of state (for example, Côte d'Ivoire).

In settings beset by armed conflict, the social contract is weakened and fragmented. Subgroups may form agreements along regional or identity dimensions in competition with the state, and hence local social contracts become stronger than ones at the level of the national government. Sometimes these local contracts can have positive outcomes, such as in Somaliland (Phillips 2020), but more often they lead to the breakup of the social fabric, such as in Sierra Leone and Liberia in the 1990s and early 2000s.

Two types of contracts (what has been called a dual citizenship) that may be in competition are observed: (1) within the local community, ethnic, or religious identity; and (2) between those groups and the state (Leonard, Mushi, and Vincent 2011). When armed conflict fractures along identity lines, for example, around religion or language (Fisiy 2019), those identity loyalties may be stronger than allegiance to the state. In turn, armed groups may begin to offer more effective governance arrangements that can be coercive but also reciprocal in nature. Armed groups such as al-Shabaab extort taxes but also provide justice and customary dispute resolution (Ahmad 2019).

Two other aspects of the social contract are important to note. First is the nature of the bargain between armed forces and political power, which often leads to a conflation of the two and military leaders assume political power.

The second is the intermediary role of international partners and their relation-ship with the state. Here the social contract, even enshrined in a compact, may be more important to the state than the state's relationship with citizens given the access to international aid and legitimacy (Ahmad 2019).

What does this understanding mean for development actors? Supporting a social contract in conflict settings requires ongoing explicit and implicit nego-tiations between different interest groups and a range of formal and informal power holders. This process is where the links between peacemaking, media-tion, peacebuilding, and development are found. As highlighted by the United Nations–World Bank partnership, sustained engagement is critical, given how those negotiations can remain unresponsive and unstable (United Nations and World Bank 2019). Where this study and the recent literature (Kaplan 2014; McCandless 2019) seem to converge is on the normative policy aspects of using the social contract, and in particular the focus on three critical areas:

- The first area is the inclusiveness of the social contract, and specifically the inclu-siveness of the political settlement. Mediation and negotiation are not usually seen as the preserve of the World Bank but more for the diplomatic community or specific arms of the United Nations system. However, underlying the bargain-ing of many political settlements are socioeconomic issues (revenue sharing, nat-ural resources, land, lagging regions) to which development institutions such as the World Bank can lend their technical expertise. Recovery and Peacebuilding Assessments,[3] as well as the work on national dialogues, are examples of how development actors can scale up this kind of support to broaden the political settlement beyond the immediacy of elite power sharing.

- The second area concerns responsiveness and the effective and inclusive delivery of services by institutions. In some respects, the World Bank has made great strides in integrating social inclusion into its policies and opera-tions, particularly with regard to gender, disability, indigenous persons, and lesbian, gay, bisexual, transgender, queer, and intersex individuals (Das and Espinoza 2020; World Bank 2013). More sensitive for the World Bank has been its ability to measure and act upon exclusions that may be of a religious- or ethnic-identity nature.

- The third area concerns civil capacity and social cohesion and the broadening and deepening of social covenants. Much of the social contract discussion focuses on vertical relations between state and citizen, whereas the conflict literature (Kaplan 2014) places an emphasis on the relative social cohesion between different groups. Although some work has been undertaken to bet-ter understand ways to measure social cohesion, it could be argued that very few resources are devoted to peacebuilding, intergroup mediation, and the building of platforms for collective action.

The real challenge for the World Bank in a fragmented contract, such as dur-ing an armed conflict, is that as a lending institution primarily for governments it can be perceived to be acting in a one-sided manner. The institution has begun to focus on civil capacity along with its focus on citizen engagement, albeit the record here is mixed (World Bank 2018). However, its resourcing for civil society institutions remains so small[4] that it could continue to be seen as working only through one side of the social contract.

African Protests and Reshaping the Social Contract

Protests are an important bargaining mechanism through which large groups of citizens can demonstrate their political weight, and 2019 has been referred to as the year of global street protests and mass demonstrations (Rachman 2019). In their geographical coverage, the protests were unrivaled in scope and variety, with comparisons often made to 1989 and even to the waves of insurgency in 1948. Typically seen as cases of "insurgent" or "street" citizenship (Giugni and Grasso 2019; Holston 2009), the protests were on a scale capable of radically disrupting daily life and inducing panic measures from governments as far afield as Algeria; Bolivia; Chile; Colombia; the Czech Republic; Ecuador; France; Hong Kong SAR, China; India; Iraq; the Islamic Republic of Iran; Lebanon; Malta; the Russian Federation; Spain; and Sudan (Brannen, Haig, and Schmidt 2020). Popular mobilization across such disparate locations, coupled with their variety of political repertoires, goals, and forms of organization, defy easy generalization. But their impact is not in question. Street protests and strikes saw Evo Morales, the president of Bolivia, forced from office in November 2019 after 13 years in power, and presidents Abdelaziz Bouteflika of Algeria and Omar al-Bashir of Sudan both fell in April 2019 after decades in office.

Africa was no exception to the global pattern of protests, and in many respects, demonstrations there proliferated more quickly and more widely than in other regions. In 2019, there were 10,793 demonstrations in Africa according to the Armed Conflict Location and Event Data Project, compared with 819 in 2009.[5] This growth did not come out of nowhere—Africa witnessed the largest increase in antigovernment protests in the world in the decade since 2010, increasing by 23.8 percent each year (more than twice the global average) and increasing by 746 percent over the decade (Brannen, Haig, and Schmidt 2020). Armed violence and fatalities increased in Africa after 2010, largely accounted for by insurgencies in the Central African Republic, the Democratic Republic of Congo, Nigeria, Somalia, South Sudan, and Sudan (though decreasing since 2014 as part of a longer term downward trend). The number of fatalities per protest, however, has declined steadily from 2001, from nine per event to fewer than three (Ciliers 2018).

During earlier waves of protests, demonstrations typically endured for days or weeks, but in recent cases, in Guinea, Malawi, Sudan, and Togo, for example, they have continued for many months. Especially large mobilizations occurred during 2019 in Cameroon, the Democratic Republic of Congo, Ethiopia, Kenya, Nigeria, South Africa, South Sudan, and Sudan, typically triggered by highly localized events. Ethiopia was rocked by mass street protests across its Oromia and Amhara regions over grievances about political exclusion. In South Africa, large-scale and persistent student unrest at virtually all university campuses over fees, hiring, and curriculum significantly disrupted the academic year. Highly contested elections saw widespread protests erupt in the Democratic Republic of Congo, Gabon, and Uganda and even in countries—Angola, Chad, and Zimbabwe—where the public and political spheres are tightly regulated. Protests in Malawi against the reelection of the incumbent president in May 2019 led to the Constitutional Court in February ordering a rerun, only the second time judges have done so in African history, following Kenya's example in 2017. Underlying all of these movements is the larger question of what full citizenship should entail and the validity of the social contract. Protests question the contract's tacit and common agreements—in short, its legitimacy and authority—on what citizens expect from the state and the state's capacity and willingness to deliver on these expectations.

According to survey data, the average age of protestors is 35 years and protesters are likely to be male, urban, and educated. Roughly 10 percent of those surveyed by Afrobarometer across the continent (2002–15) had participated in a protest in the preceding 12 months (South Africa is the extreme outlier, where the comparable figure is more than 18 percent). The occupational profile of protestors, however, is complex: informal sector workers, domestic workers, and farmers make up a significant proportion of protestors. Africa's youth, particularly those residing in urban areas, operate in ways broadly similar to their counterparts in other regions of the world. In comparison with their older compatriots (Resnick and Casale 2011), even though youth vote less, they are more likely to demonstrate an attachment to opposition parties rather than any affinity to incumbent parties.

Since 2010, protests have arisen across the continent for a variety of reasons. In some cases, the cause proved to be flawed elections (Senegal in 2011), in others the price of oil (Nigeria in 2012), in some instances the abject failure of local government to deliver basic services (South Africa in 2012), and in others ethnic exclusion (Ethiopia in 2016). Survey data covering the period 2012–15 for South Africa (Lancaster 2006; Matebesi 2017), the country with the largest number of protests and highest participation rate, suggest that labor, crime and policing, service provision, housing, transport, and education triggered two-thirds of all protests, with a marked contrast between rural and urban protests (in rural areas corruption, land, water, and jobs predominated). More generally, however, corruption figures quite centrally in protest motivation. The 2019 Transparency International global corruption barometer for Africa shows that more than half of respondents felt that corruption was on the rise, that one in four surveyed had paid a bribe in the previous year for public service access, and that the police and government officials are seen as the most corrupt institutions.[6] Survey data from individuals across more than 30 African countries taken from the 2005–06 and 2014–16 surveys reveals that a respondent who has the highest experience of paying bribes will have a 40 percent probability of taking part in anticorruption demonstrations (Transparency International 2019).

The nonviolent overthrow of the heads of state in Algeria and Sudan in 2019 are not aberrations and point to a number of continental trends for which the changing profile of social protests is a crucial indicator. First is the democratic opening of the 1990s. The move to institute free and fair elections, to remove authoritarian and in some cases dictatorial leaders, and to reform the "gatekeeper states" that controlled access to foreign aid, receipts from natural resource exports, and taxes on trade has certainly been slow, laborious, and uneven, but the gains were evident, clearing a space within which protest movements could both operate and grow. The spillover effects of the Arab Spring reverberated across the continent even though social protests had begun much earlier.[7]

Second is a growing commitment across the continent to democratic norms and forms. In an Afrobarometer poll of 34 countries published in 2019, 68 percent of Africans said that democracy was the best form of government, a share that had been broadly stable over the previous decade. The figure is higher when respondents are presented with specific alternatives; 78 percent, for example, said they would not give up multiparty elections for strongman rule. Across Africa, the demand for democracy is outstripping supply, and young, urban populations in particular want the right to express themselves, to vote in fair elections, and to hold leaders to account.

Third, since 2000 most demonstrations and protests in Africa have been unarmed and peaceful. Since 2011, mass uprisings in Africa have accounted for one in three of the nonviolent campaigns aiming to topple dictatorships around the world, almost twice as many as in Asia. Africa's nonviolent uprisings have, moreover, had the highest success rate in the world: more than half of the uprisings aimed at overthrowing dictatorships have succeeded, in countries as diverse as Burkina Faso, Côte d'Ivoire, Madagascar, Mali, Niger, South Africa, Tunisia, Zambia, and, most recently, Algeria and Sudan. This far surpasses the success rate for movements against autocratic regimes in all other regions. Some commentators, in fact, claim that rising "people power" across the continent is doing what global arrest warrants cannot (Marks, Chenoweth, and Okeke 2019).

Importantly, the growth of protest movements does not signal a linear pattern of positive change. Depending on a wide range of factors, protests and their aftermath can and do take multiple pathways. Protests are sometimes framed as disruptive: protestors are troublemakers and destabilizers rather than heroic or constructive actors. Peaceful protests can, and do, turn violent: of the 2,880 protests in South Africa between 2013 and 2015, 53 percent involved violence. Mass mobilizations can disrupt economic activity, and losses of revenue, property, and life may be substantial. Protests and social movements frequently achieve little except a ferocious backlash by security forces. Recent prodemocracy movements in Cameroon and Togo have so far led only to violent government crackdowns. And even when civil resistance works in the short term, the new system sometimes falls short of delivering real change. In South Africa, for example, the explosion of community protests after 2009[8] was matched by deepening corruption within both the African National Congress and the government, producing a national debate over "state capture." Where popular upheavals have toppled dictators, a second wave of counterrevolutionary forces has mobilized against the new order, as with the popular coup that installed Abdel Fattah el-Sisi as president in the Arab Republic of Egypt. In Zimbabwe, since the November 2017 protests that helped drive President Robert Mugabe from office, the military has tightened control. As leaders of the Zimbabwe African National Union–Patriotic Front moved to take power and impede the democratic transition, repression increased against activists, forcing many to lie low and move away from opposition politics.

Most African countries display what has been called "electoral authoritarianism" or "violent democracy" (Miller 2013), in which the pageantry of voting obscures a lack of genuine democratic practice. Elections are regular but regularly rigged and often marked by political thuggery and intimidation. And in some respects, the picture seems to have deteriorated. Freedom House (2020) classifies just seven countries in Africa as "free" (the lowest total since 1990). A closing of the public space in some places is apparent in new Afrobarometer survey data, which show that Africans who say they are free to say what they think declined from 79 percent in 2008 to 70 percent in 2018. From 2004 to 2018, 12 African countries passed laws making it harder for nongovernmental organizations to operate and more are planning to do so, all aided and abetted by the ability to regulate social media platforms. Of the 21 countries that shut down the internet in 2019, 12 were African. There may be an emergent "democratic divide" between those more open and partially democratic regimes, which shift and morph under popular pressures, and the authoritarian regimes, which, in the face of opposition, turn the repressive screws (Cheeseman 2015).

Social protests can and do continue under such circumstances. For a younger generation of city dwellers—the nascent middle classes, educated youths, women's organizations—democratic backsliding will be contested. Protests cannot always restrain a determined autocrat, but they can challenge repressive power, which explains in part the rise in the number of peaceful, if not always democratic, changes of government. There have been 29 nonviolent transfers of power since 2015 (as of 2020), compared with just 9 in the first half of the decade. Of the 49 African leaders as heads of state at the start of 2015, only 22 are in place as of 2020. Even African legislatures, typically dismissed as rubber-stamping devices, have sometimes bowed to popular pressure by helping ensure that, since 1990, all but 7 of the 47 countries in Africa that have nonceremonial heads of state have term limits.[9] These limits are more than twice as likely to be kept as broken. Protests, mass mobilizations, and armed militancy can shift the political dial, even if the postprotest trajectories appear varied and their consequences contradictory.

In some cases, single goal–oriented movements (for example, popular protests over the price of bread) may simply evaporate overnight when the norm of a just price is reestablished. In 2012, protests against removal of oil subsidies in Nigeria succeeded in keeping prices low, but at the same time left the system and its corrupt elite beneficiaries intact. Malawi provides an illustration in which civil society groups and popular protest have periodically acted as a sort of political thermostat, successfully limiting egregious attempts by the president to subvert democracy yet doing little to change the overall incentives and responsiveness of those in power. In Senegal, the two most important of several movements directed toward democracy and human rights—Y'en a Marre and M-23[10]—reveal quite different pathways and trajectories. M-23 focused on regime-related constitutional and political problems whereas Y'en a Marre strategically folded bread and butter and service issues into their messages and organization. M-23 was ultimately absorbed (perhaps coopted) into government; Y'en a Marre entered a phase of radicalization and grew its support base, establishing satellite organizations engaged in civic education and vocational training. Whereas M-23 lost legitimacy, Y'en a Marre became a powerful force capable of turning out diverse and mobilized constituencies and promoting reformist agendas while retaining autonomy.

Finally, there is South Africa and its vital tradition of local and community protests, especially since 2010. Pravin Gordhan, who was summarily dismissed as minister of finance in 2017, observed that the African National Congress has "moved away from [its] duty to serve our people […] We have broken that contract."[11] Municipal protests escalated in 2007 and subsequently reached unprecedented levels (there were, on average, roughly 375 protests annually between 2009 and 2017). Service delivery protests constituted 80 percent of the total and were wide ranging, addressing schooling, roads, housing, and water provision. The 2016 local government elections brought to power a new coalition of opposition parties in several municipalities that had experienced the largest protests. Although it is too early to evaluate the impact of the coalition-led municipalities on service delivery, it seems plausible to conclude that the subsequent election of President Cyril Ramaphosa was not unrelated to the popular protests emerging from below. If the 2019 elections were a referendum about rescuing South Africa (LeBas 2013; Riedl 2014), these protests arguably were instrumental in resisting the decay in the country's social contract.

There is no ready-made template of prescriptive policy measures that can be derived from Africa's growing role in the rise of global protests and mass demonstration. Ultimately, what is key is the extent to which protests are linked to or contribute to opposition parties or more extensive forms of institutionalized politics capable of not only advancing democracy (LeBas 2013; Riedl 2014) but also of enhancing state responsiveness and state capabilities, and therefore state legitimacy, which is at the heart of the social contract. It is not easy to predict which protests are likely to succeed in doing so. If much of the research on the third-wave protests is correct, then the significance of cross-class and cross-generational alliances and the intersection of middle-class leadership under conditions of limited upward mobility (economic pessimism) can help identify conditions under which sustained popular mobilization might occur. Synergies between communities and local or provincial government have also proven generative, for example, the community protests for better local government service provision in South Africa.

Normative Aspects of Social Contracts: The Case of Human Rights[12]

Citizen-state relations, viewed through the prism of the social contract, invariably invoke the human rights construct as the enabling framework. In the midst of the multiplicity of influences that contribute to the shaping of social contracts in the African context, including the prevalent characteristics of sociocultural variance, developmental asymmetry, and legal pluralism, the human rights paradigm presents a constant pillar for both benchmarking and assessing the progress of the state in addressing the welfare of the governed. Human rights enter the social contract framework mainly through the responsiveness outcome because many of the fundamental rights concern freedom of expression and protection from violent repression such as torture and political killings.

Human rights have an important normative component (Bentley 2019). As Ozar explains, "when we say someone has a right of some sort, we are … talking about what ought or ought not to be done. Rights talk is one kind of moral discourse. It is used to inform people of their obligations and to give explanations of our own and others' choices and actions" (Ozar 1986, 4). Based on this definition, all human rights would then have some normative element to them. They are not necessarily about what empirically is; they are about what morally ought to be. It is important to bear this in mind when discussing human rights generally, but in Africa in particular, where the gap between the rights that are declared and their realization in practice can seem impossibly daunting.

Second, Ozar (1986) observes that insofar as rights inevitably generate obligations on the part of others to respect or honor those rights, all rights imply relations between people in the course of their exercise. As Ozar (1986, 6) puts it, "a right is a relationship; it is a relationship between a person who has the right and others who have corresponding obligations to act or to refrain." So human rights then, consisting as they do of a set of normative standards that create duties for others, in particular the state of which one is either a resident or a citizen, set the parameters of a particular kind of relationship between the citizen and the state. Where human rights set the normative standard, or requirements for the state, they act as a bulwark against the encroachment of the state on the individual in various ways, but they also create requirements for the state in how it ought to function in delivering services, using public funds, and managing natural resources.

Three enabling factors need to be in place to shift the bargaining power to embed human rights and strengthen the social contract in African contexts: (1) interactive procedures to resolve conflicts and hold the state to account; (2) an inclusive environment that allows for unfettered participation, including that of civil society organizations; and (3) representation that is empowering, inclusive, and accountable. These factors are illustrated, respectively, in the relevant in-depth sectoral study (Bentley 2019) through the examples of the Life Healthcare Esidimeni tragedy in South Africa, proposed legislation designed to hobble civil society organizations that aim to defend the rights of communities in the oil-rich areas of Uganda, and the decentralization process and the demand for directly elected local officials in Ghana.

Inequality, the Social Contract, and Electoral Support

A World Bank report on the social contract in the Europe and Central Asia region (Bussolo et al. 2018) stresses the importance of redistribution and taxation for both reducing inequality and broadly enhancing the welfare of citizens. It warns that the persistence of high inequality because of one's social background and ethnicity may weaken popular support for the market economy and the implicit social contract accompanying it (IEG 2019). A vibrant social contract—in which citizens share a strong sense of collective solidarity and purpose and broadly trust that private resources they relinquish to the state will be spent on public goods and services benefiting society as a whole—imbues both taxation and redistribution policies with greater political support. The realization of these goods and services themselves reinforces the vibrancy of the social contract. Inequality takes a predominant place in the social contract framework presented in this report given that it is one of the main components of the inclusiveness dimension.

What are the large patterns of support for those policies in different parts of the world, and in Africa, specifically? Piketty (2018) analyzes voting patterns in support of both taxation and redistribution in Western countries. He notes that previous support patterns between the left-wing and right-wing political parties have changed away from class-based identities. Traditionally, lower-income citizens with less education tended to vote for socialist, labor, and democratic parties favoring higher shares of taxation and redistribution, and citizens with higher incomes and more education increasingly voted for more conservative parties favoring the status quo. Analyzing some European countries and the United States, he states that these patterns seem to no longer hold. Instead, there seems to be a new cleavage between cultural elites who vote for left-leaning parties and business elites who vote for right-wing parties. People with lower education and incomes feel abandoned and turn to populist parties.

This structural change explains why there has not been a sufficiently strong electoral push against policies that exacerbate inequalities. The social contract seems to have weakened in Western countries. Discussing political ideologies in Africa in the early 1970s, Graham (1972) focuses on two main historic political ideologies: Pan-Africanism, that is, an assertion of black identity; and African socialism, that is, an attempt to apply traditional communitarian values to nation-building. The presence of these ideologies explains why Conroy-Krutz and Lewis (2011) highlight an important distinction from Western politics. In Africa, they write, "candidate appeals on the basis of what Western observers would call ideology are rare in contemporary Africa" (Conroy-Krutz and Lewis 2011, iii). In their study of African politics, they find that major parties are not distinguishable from one another with regard to their adherents' attitudes toward the proper role of the state in the economy. Their findings hold for all African "countries included in the analyses and are consistent across subgroups" (Conroy-Krutz and Lewis 2011, iii). Conroy-Krutz and Lewis cite an example from the 2011 elections in Uganda in which the candidates called for adoption of federalism in the country, which would enhance the power of traditional rulers. However, the same candidates who made federalism a central part of their platforms also "advocated for a significant expansion of government-run programs on health, job creation, education, infrastructure and tourism" (Conroy-Krutz and Lewis 2011, 1), funded and overseen by the central government. The authors argue that such is the norm throughout Africa.

Atta Mills (2018) supports that conclusion, citing an example from Ghana. In his paper, he writes about Ghana's largely free and fair elections, which are vigorously contested. Although the biggest parties have similar ideologies on paper (the National Democratic Congress claims social democracy whereas the New Patriotic Party is liberal democratic), they differ mostly on their geographic support base and cannot draw support from any identifiable socioeconomic group. Atta Mills concludes that "party supporters appear to be no more than associations of prominent individuals and their followers or 'fan clubs.'" The absence of opposing ideology-based governing platforms has led to a situation in which the administrations of both parties avoid imposing negative impacts on organized labor and prefer indirect taxation for mobilizing domestic resources. As a result, the tax-to-GDP ratio is very low in Ghana, while economic rents from the extractive industry are an important source of government revenue. The highly visible and lucrative infrastructure projects are mostly financed through foreign (sovereign) loans, government bond issues, and public-private partnerships. Social tensions are heightened because of high unemployment and indebtedness. Inequality is increasing. Atta Mills (2018) concludes that Africa needs political parties that are more inclusive and reflect the socioeconomic aspirations of broad segments of the population. Despite the finding of Rothstein, Samanni, and Teorell (2012) that poor governments undermine trust in state institutions and thereby decrease popular support for state-sponsored redistribution, previously inactive socioeconomic groups need to find their voices and demand representation and reforms that can lead to reductions of both poverty and inequality. For the social contract to hold, elites should be made more accountable to their citizens—by protecting open media, promoting greater civic participation, and conducting regular performance audits.

Social Accountability and the Social Contract

The *World Development Report 2004: Making Services Work for Poor People* (World Bank 2004) helped put social accountability into mainstream development practice by making citizen and civil society agency a critical factor in improving public policy and service delivery through accountable government. This effort has led to interest among practitioners and scholars alike in the relationship between social accountability and the social contract between citizens and the state. The creation in 2012 of the Global Partnership for Social Accountability (GPSA)[13] in the World Bank, for example, was inspired by a view of the Arab Spring as manifesting a citizen-led critique of a failed social contract, and a desire for its renewal in which social accountability would be an important instrument for change.[14] (See box 5.1.) Although this rationale was not informed by empirical study, it strongly suggested the potential utility of a social contract frame in understanding citizen-state relationships, aided by social accountability practice. In fact, immediately following the Arab Spring in 2011, the World Bank awarded a US$500,000 grant to support formation of the Affiliated Network for Social Accountability in the Arab World, a regional network for advancing social accountability practice, as a signal of this move.[15]

BOX 5.1

Social Accountability and the Social Contract—A View from 2011

"Two weeks ago, we convened a conference at the World Bank to listen to Arab voices—youth groups, women's groups, change agents.

"What do they want? They want opportunity, justice, a job. They want rules and laws that are fair, predictable, and transparent. They want food and shelter for their families, good schools for their children, and neighborhoods that are safe. They want police forces that are protectors, not predators; they want governments that can be trusted. They want voice, and accountability—and they want it in villages, towns, and neighborhoods. They want a say over public services that have been so contorted so that they are neither open to the public nor offer real service. They want information and the right to know, and to participate.

"*They want a new social contract* [emphasis added]. They want dignity. They want respect. And if they are women, they want these same things.

"There are some in this audience who will say: Yes, that may be what they want, but that's politics not economics. I am here to say: Some of that may be what we think of as politics, but most of it is also what we know is good economics; most of it is what we know is good for fighting corruption; most of it is what we know is good for inclusive and sustainable development."

Source: Zoellick 2011.

Yet, above all, it is the progression in social accountability theory and practice since the *World Development Report 2004* that makes it a potentially useful companion to the social contract framework. In the *World Development Report 2004*, social accountability is understood as an approach to public governance that involves citizens and civil society organizations (CSOs) in the management of public resources, in public decision-making and problem-solving, and in holding government accountable for its actions, including good-quality public service delivery (Bousquet et al. 2012). Today, "second-generation" social accountability theory and practice are closely aligned with the social contract framework presented in this report and its resonance with the notion of citizen-state bargaining in *World Development Report 2017: Governance and the Law*. Social accountability theory has a clear strategic advantage in informing, supporting, or even evaluating social contracts. There are clear pointers in this report to the significance of social accountability to the social contract frame, including references to citizen-led accountability, that is, citizens' capacity to hold the state to account for its commitments, and civil capacity associated with collective problem solving.

This relationship with social accountability is manifested in the following specific areas:

- *Collaborative social accountability counterbalances the Bank's otherwise one-sided relationship with governments.* It mitigates the perception of the Bank as working only one side of the social contract. As an example, even as the World Bank lends to the government of Ghana, a GPSA grant to the CSO SEND Ghana supported CSO collaboration with the ministries of local government, education, and health, and supported CSO-facilitated monitoring and oversight of health and education budgets and services by local communities.

- *Collaborative social accountability can reinforce the three compasses this report argues are related to the cross-section of social contracts in Africa.* First, the GPSA's collaborative model has the advantage of being embedded in the World Bank's compacts with governments, which helps facilitate state responsiveness.[16] Through diverse participatory mechanisms (social audits, community scorecards and citizen report cards, qualitative and quantitative surveys, participatory budgeting, tracking of citizen entitlements from the state, or facilitation of state-citizen interfaces and dialogues), social accountability processes work to make state provision of services respond meaningfully to citizen needs and preferences. Second, social accountability has direct implications for the second compass, imposing binding constraints on the citizen-state bargain, which depends on mapping and addressing civil and state capacities. The GPSA has validated the salience of these capacities with partners in Africa.[17] Equipping and empowering societal and state actors with appropriate skills is also vital to managing expectations, mitigating grievances, and encouraging more effective public management that can strengthen the social contract.[18] Third, social accountability can inform the third compass on social contract outcomes. From gender budgeting and participatory budgeting experiments across the regions to social audits and service-related scorecards, social accountability practice has been shown to support positive development outcomes. In Bangladesh, a GPSA-supported CSO coalition collaborated with local governments (union parishads, or UPs) and facilitated the participation of local communities in UPs' plans and budgets. This enabled UPs to meet the requirements of the 2009 Local Government Act for the statutory block grant allocation (which contained targets for inclusion of women's priorities).

- *Collaborative social accountability, relational state-building, and state legitimacy.* Most discussions on strengthening the social contract rely on an assumption that improved state-led service delivery to populations will automatically increase state legitimacy. An important feature of collaborative social accountability is its ability to make citizens' experiences of the state meaningful through feedback to the state and facilitated in-depth participation and co-creation. It enhances the quality and inclusiveness of the process throughout the service delivery chain. This experience is considered to be key to increasing state legitimacy in the eyes of citizens.

- *Collaborative social accountability has the potential to strengthen social contracts in settings of fragility, conflict, and violence and to support conflict prevention and transformation.* The GPSA and its partners have been experimenting with this collaborative approach across the humanitarian, peace, and development nexus, and have begun to produce important operational insights into applying this approach in hard places. The tools and processes of social accountability have demonstrated the ability to address all of these issues and more. Collaborative social accountability can be an avenue for addressing societal grievances and mediating citizen-state dynamics (Grandvoinnet, Aslam, and Raha 2015) in settings of fragility, conflict, and violence. A GPSA-supported social accountability multistakeholder platform in Gorno-Badakhshan, Tajikistan, for example, facilitated direct policy engagement by disenfranchised youth on jobs with government authorities, fostering a sense of belonging.

Response to COVID-19

The utility of the social contract to understanding the behavior of states and citizens has also come to prominence with the onset of the COVID-19 pandemic. The pandemic has triggered the first recession in Africa in 25 years, with growth forecast between −2.1 percent and −5.1 percent in 2020 from a modest 2.4 percent in 2019 (Zeufack et al. 2020). Because of the economic downturn and the legacy of increased public debt, the fiscal space for states to be able to respond to the primary public health impacts of the pandemic, let alone the secondary impacts of the social and economic lockdown, is limited. Africa paid US$35.8 billion in total debt service in 2018, 2.1 percent of regional GDP. In turn, it is estimated that the pandemic could cost the region between US$37 billion and US$79 billion in output losses for 2020. The impact on household welfare is expected to be significant, with welfare losses in the optimistic scenario projected to reach 7 percent in 2020, compared with a nonpandemic scenario (Zeufack et al. 2020). In a region where roughly 8 out of 10 people are engaged in low-productivity informal employment and often just making ends meet, the livelihoods of millions of households, and their human capital, are at risk. A combination of the pandemic, a locust outbreak, the global downturn, and armed conflict is going to have a significant impact on food security in a number of countries in Africa. According to the Food and Agriculture Organization,

239 million people are already undernourished (FAO, IFAD, UNICEF, WFP, and WHO 2021) and agricultural production may contract between 2.6 percent and 7 percent. Food imports would decline substantially (as much as 25 percent or as little as 13 percent) from a combination of higher transaction costs, reduced domestic demand, and export bans in the wake of the pandemic (Ehui 2020).

The pandemic is affecting countries in different ways but straining the social contract across the board. Certain West African countries, notably Guinea, Liberia, and Sierra Leone, have learned important lessons from the Ebola crisis and have swiftly executed prevention measures adapted to the local context and that are less expensive than many measures taken elsewhere (Richards 2020). Oil-revenue-dependent states, including Angola, Chad, Nigeria, and South Sudan, have suffered additional fiscal shocks with the rapid decrease in prices due to the global downturn (Campbell 2020). For conflict-affected countries, there are fears of cascading impacts from constrained peacekeeping, hindrances on a security presence, and an increase in armed group activity that, in turn, could increase the humanitarian impacts on vulnerable populations, particularly in the Sahel and the Horn of Africa (Bryant 2020).

In this context, the COVID-19 pandemic has made concepts pertinent to the social contract ever more salient, in particular in relation to the role of the state, the resilience of institutions, and the relationship between the state and its citizens. As social distancing measures have been executed, including stay-at-home and curfew orders, not only has the capability of the state been seen as important but so has the trust of its citizens (Fukuyama 2020). Given that the secondary impacts of COVID-19 are going to be equally if not more harmful to vulnerable populations, good communications, consent, and community engagement will be critical to ensuring an effective state policy response (de Waal 2020). Furthermore, not only are vertical relations between citizens and the state essential, but so is social cohesion among different groups in society (Soyemi 2020).

The pandemic further highlights a number of common development challenges that many African countries face, although they often manifest themselves in varying ways. These challenges include modest growth rates, high levels of poverty, armed conflict, inequality, systematic weaknesses in institutions, and challenges in the delivery of quality services. This plethora of common challenges, plus migration and forced displacement, economic integration and technological change, the climate crisis, rapid urbanization (more than half of Africa's population will live in cities by 2040), and a youth bulge in many countries (11 million youth annually will enter the labor market over the next decade), adds complexity for policy makers. These complexities often render old business-as-usual ways to tackle development obsolete. At the same time, the fiscal space is tightening and the urgency of expanding domestic revenue mobilization brings issues of governance and citizen-state relations to the fore.

Notes

1. Collected taxes being one of the possible sources of revenue for a government.
2. Tax data from World Development Indicators.
3. "Recovery and Peacebuilding Assessments (RPBA): FAQs" (https://www.worldbank .org/en/topic/fragilityconflictviolence/brief/recovery-peacebuilding-assessments -faqs).
4. See, for example, the Global Partnership for Social Accountability (www.thegpsa.org).
5. See "Recent Trends in Political Violence and Protests In Africa" (https://acleddata .com/2018/03/12/recent-trends-in-political-violence-protests-in-africa/); and *The Economist*, March 5, 2020, "Young Africans Want More Democracy" (https://www .economist.com/middle-east-and-africa/2020/03/05/young-africans-want-more -democracy).
6. See "What's behind the Wave of Protests in Africa?" Afrobarometer (https:// afrobarometer.org/blogs/whats-behind-wave-protests-africa).
7. Branch and Mampilly (2015) show that between 2005 and 2014 more than 90 popular protests occurred in 40 African states (not counting labor strikes and local labor strikes), and yet it was only when the revolts broke out in North Africa that Western media began to pay attention.
8. "Community protests refer to collective actions that take place within a highly localised geographic area, such as an informal shack settlement or a section of a township. They are popularly labelled as 'service delivery protests,' in reference to common demands for services such as water and electricity" (Paret 2015, 121).
9. *The Economist*, March 5, 2020, "Young Africans Want More Democracy" (https:// www.economist.com/middle-east-and-africa/2020/03/05/young-africans-want -more-democracy).
10. "Y'en a Marre" means "We're fed up." "M-23," or Mouvement du 23-Juin au Sénégal, is a coalition of political parties and civil society organizations, created in 2011, that mobilized against President Abdoulaye Wade's candidacy for a third term in 2012.
11. "Constitution Is a Social Contract—Gordhan," *News 24*, April 4, 2016 (https://www .news24.com/News24/constitution-is-a-social-contract-gordhan-20160404).
12. The spotlight presented here is taken from background papers prepared for the report by Ordor (2020) and Bentley (2019); the work was financed by the Nordic Trust Fund.
13. The World Bank established the GPSA in 2012 with the purpose of bridging the gap between what citizens want and what governments actually do, enhancing citizens' voice, and, just as important, supporting the capacity of governments to respond effectively to their voice.
14. Zoellick (2011) and World Bank (2012).
15. The funding agreement was signed by World Bank Group President Robert B. Zoellick and Director of Governance and Civic Engagement, CARE-Egypt, Amr Lashin, September 22, 2011.
16. State responsiveness in this context is linked more to state response to citizen demands for better services than actions associated with macro-level "civic space," which require much more complex interventions.

17. See evaluation reports for GPSA programs in the Democratic Republic of Congo and Ghana; and the GPSA partnership with Public Sector Accountability Monitor at Rhodes University, South Africa.
18. The government of Ghana has a directorate for social accountability in its Ministry of Local Government and Rural Development that mediates government–civil society engagement and citizen oversight of government programs.

References

African Natural Resources Center. 2016. *Botswana's Mineral Revenues, Expenditure and Savings Policy: A Case Study*. Abidjan: African Development Bank Group.

Ahmad, A. 2019. "Somalia Case Study." Unpublished, World Bank, Washington, DC.

Allingham, M. G., and A. Sandmo. 1972. "Income Tax Evasion: A Theoretical Analysis." *Journal of Public Economics* 1 (3–4): 323–38.

Arrobas, D. L., K. L. Hund, M. S. McCormick, J. Ningthoujam, and J. R. Drexhage. 2017. *The Growing Role of Minerals and Metals for a Low Carbon Future*. Washington, DC: World Bank Group.

Atta Mills, C. 2018. "Politics, Policy and Implementation: The Ghanaian Paradox." Brookings Institution, Washington, DC. https://www.brookings.edu/blog/africa-in -focus/2018/07/18/politics-policy-and-implementation-the-ghanaian-paradox/.

Beegle, K. G., A. Coudouel, M. Monsalve, and W. Mercedes. 2018. *Realizing the Full Potential of Social Safety Nets in Africa*. Washington, DC: World Bank Group.

Bentley, K. 2019. "Background Paper on Human Rights, the Social Contract and Development." Unpublished, World Bank, Washington, DC.

Berdal, M. R., and D. M. Malone. 2000. *Greed and Grievance: Economic Agendas in Civil Wars*. Boulder, CO: Lynne Rienner Publishers.

Beresford, A., M. E. Berry, and L. Mann. 2018. "Liberation Movements and Stalled Democratic Transitions: Reproducing Power in Rwanda and South Africa through Productive Liminality." *Democratization* 25 (7): 1231–50. https://doi.org/10.1080/135 10347.2018.1461209.

Bousquet, F., J. Thindwa, M. Felicio, and H. Grandvoinnet. 2012. *Supporting Social Accountability in the Middle East and North Africa: Lessons from Transitions*. Washington, DC: World Bank.

Branch, A., and Z. Mampilly. 2015. *Africa Uprising: Popular Protest and Political Change*. London: Zed Books Ltd.

Brannen, S., C. Haig, and K. Schmidt. 2020. *The Age of Mass Protests: Understanding an Escalating Global Trend*. Washington, DC: Center for Strategic and International Studies.

Bryant, L. 2020. "Africa's Conflict-Ridden Regions Face Another Existential Threat in COVID-19." Small War Journal, April 4, 2020.

Bussolo, M., M. E. Dávalos, V. Peragine, and R. Sundaram. 2018. *Toward a New Social Contract: Taking On Distributional Tensions in Europe and Central Asia*. Washington, DC: World Bank.

Campbell, J. 2020. "Africa Confronts Falling Oil Prices amid Coronavirus." Council on Foreign Relations blog, March 6, 2020. https://www.cfr.org/blog/africa-confronts-falling-oil-prices-amid-coronavirus.

Carpenter, S., R. Mallett, and R. Slater. 2012. "Social Protection and Basic Services in Fragile and Conflict-Affected Situations." Working Paper 8, Secure Livelihoods Research Consortium, Overseas Development Institute, London.

Cheeseman, N. 2015. *Democracy in Africa: Successes, Failures, and the Struggle for Political Reform*. London: Cambridge University Press.

Choi, J., M. A. Dutz, and Z. Usman. 2020. *The Future of Work in Africa: Harnessing the Potential of Digital Technologies for All*. Washington, DC: World Bank.

Ciliers, J. 2018. *Violence in Africa*. Pretoria: Institute for Security Studies.

Collier, P., and A. Hoeffler. 2004. "Greed and Grievance in Civil War." *Oxford Economic Papers* 56 (4): 563–95.

Conroy-Krutz, J., and D. Lewis. 2011. "Mapping Ideologies in African Landscapes." Working Paper 129, Afrobarometer. https://www.files.ethz.ch/isn/128199/AfropaperNo129_2.pdf.

Cosbey, A., H. Mann, N. Maennling, P. Toledano, J. Geipel, and M. D. Brauch. 2016. *Mining a Mirage? Reassessing the Shared-Value Paradigm in Light of the Technological Advances in the Mining Sector*. Manitoba: International Institute for Sustainable Development.

Cust, J., and A. Zeufack. Forthcoming. "The Dog that Didn't Bark: The Missed Opportunity of Africa's Resource Boom." Policy Research Working Paper Series, World Bank, Washington, DC.

Das, M. B., and S. A. Espinoza. 2020. *Inclusion Matters in Africa*. Washington, DC: World Bank.

Devarajan, S. 2017. "How to Use Oil Revenues Efficiently: Universal Basic Income." Future Development, Brookings Institution, Washington, DC.

Devarajan, S., and Ianchovichina, E. 2018. "A Broken Social Contract, Not High Inequality, Led to the Arab Spring." *Review of Income and Wealth* 64 (s1): 5–25.

De Waal, A. 2020. "COVID-19: 'Know Your Epidemic, Act on its Politics.'" Reinventing Peace blog post, March 31, 2020, World Peace Foundation.

Di John, J., and J. Putzel. 2009. "Political Settlements: Issues Paper." Governance and Social Development Resource Centre. University of Birmingham, Birmingham, UK.

Dreier, S., A. Alik-Lagrange, and M. Lake. 2020. "Social Protection and the Social Contract." Unpublished, World Bank, Washington, DC.

Dreier, S., A. Alik-Lagrange, M. Lake, and A. Porisky. 2021. "Social Protection and State-Society Relations in Environments of Low and Uneven State Capacity." *Annual Review of Political Science* 24: 151–74.

Ehui, S. 2020. "Protecting Food Security in Africa during COVID-19." Africa in Focus blog post, May 14, 2020, Brookings Institution, Washington, DC.

Esteban, J., and G. Schneider. 2008. "Polarization and Conflict, Theoretical and Empirical Issues." *Journal of Peace Studies* 45 (2): 131–41.

Eubank, N. 2012. "Taxation, Political Accountability and Foreign Aid: Lessons from Somaliland." *Journal of Development Studies* 48 (4): 465–80.

FAO, IFAD, UNICEF, WFP, and WHO (Food and Agriculture Organization, International Fund for Agricultural Development, United Nations Children's Fund, World Food Programme, and World Health Organization). 2021. *The State of Food Security and Nutrition in the World 2021. Transforming Food Systems for Food Security, Improved Nutrition and Affordable Healthy Diets for All.* Rome: FAO.

Fisiy, C. 2019. "Cameroon Case Study." Unpublished, World Bank, Washington, DC.

Freedom House. 2020. *Freedom in the World.* Lanham, MD: Rowman & Littlefield. https://freedomhouse.org/report/freedom-world/2020/leaderless-struggle-democracy.

Fukuyama, F. 2020. "The Thing That Determines a Country's Resistance to the Coronavirus." *The Atlantic.* https://www.theatlantic.com/ideas/archive/2020/03/thing-determines-how-well-countries-respond-coronavirus/609025/.

Gatt, L., and O. Owen. 2018. "Direct Taxation and State-Society Relations in Lagos, Nigeria." *Development and Change* 49 (5): 1195–222.

Gentilini, U., M. Almenfi, P. Dale, J. Blomquist, H. Natarajan, G. Galicia, R. Palacios, and V. Desai. 2020. "Social Protection and Jobs Responses to COVID-19: A Real-Time Review of Country Measures." World Bank, Washington, DC.

Giugni, M., and M. T. Grasso. 2019. *Street Citizens: Protest Politics and Social Movement Activism in the Age of Globalization.* London: Cambridge University Press.

Graham, J. D. 1982. *The Centennial Review.* 16 (1): 23–40.

Grandvoinnet, H., G. Aslam, and S. Raha. 2015. *Opening the Black Box: The Contextual Drivers of Social Accountability.* New Frontiers of Social Policy. Washington, DC: World Bank.

Holston, J. 2009. *Insurgent Citizenship: Disjunctions of Democracy and Modernity in Brazil.* Princeton: Princeton University Press.

IEG (Independent Evaluation Group). 2019. *Social Contracts and World Bank Country Engagements: Lessons from Emerging Practices.* Washington, DC: World Bank.

Kaplan, S. 2014. "Social Covenants and Social Contracts in Transitions." Report, NOREF (Norwegian Peacebuilding Resource Center).

Karl, T.-L. 1997. *The Paradox of Plenty: Oil Booms and Petro States.* Berkeley, CA; London: University of California Press.

Lancaster, L. 2006. "At the Heart of Discontent: Measuring Public Violence in South Africa." ISS Working Paper 292, Institute for Security Studies, Pretoria.

LeBas, A. 2013. *From Protest to Parties: Party-Building and Democratization in Africa.* Oxford: Oxford University Press.

Leonard, D. K. 2013. "Social Contracts, Networks and Security in Tropical African Conflict States." *IDS Bulletin.*

Leonard, D. K., F. M. Mushi, and J. Vincent. 2011. "Social Contracts and Security in Sub-Saharan African Conflict States." African Studies Association.

Levi, M. 1988. *Of Rule and Revenue.* Berkeley, CA: University of California Press.

Levi, M., and L. Stoker. 2000. "Political Trust and Trustworthiness." *Annual Review of Political Science* 3 (1): 475–507. https://doi.org/10.1146/annurev.polisci.3.1.475.

Lindert, K., T. George Karippacheril, I. Rodríguez Caillava, and K. Nishikawa Chávez, eds. 2020. *Sourcebook on the Foundations of Social Protection Delivery Systems*. Washington, DC: World Bank.

Lundren, C. J., A. H. Thomas, and R. C. York. 2013. *Boom, Bust, or Prosperity? Managing Sub-Saharan Africa's Natural Resource Wealth*. African Department. Washington, DC: International Monetary Fund. https://www.imf.org/en/Publications/Departmental -Papers-Policy-Papers/Issues/2016/12/31/Boom-Bust-or-Prosperity-Managing-Sub -Saharan-Africas-Natural-Resource-Wealth-40476.

Marks, Z., E. Chenoweth, and J. Okeke. 2019. "People Power Is Rising in Africa." *Foreign Affairs*, April 2019. https://www.foreignaffairs.com/articles/africa/2019-04-25/people -power-rising-africa.

Matebesi, S. 2017. *Civil Strife against Local Governance: Dynamics of Community Protests in Contemporary South Africa*. Berlin: Barbara Budrich.

McCandless, E. 2018a. *Forging Resilient Social Contracts: A Pathway to Preventing Violent Conflict and Sustaining Peace. Summary Findings*. Oslo: United Nations Development Programme.

McCandless, E. 2019. "Forging Resilient Social Contracts." *Journal of Peacebuilding and Development* 14 (1).

Miller, M. 2013. "Electoral Authoritarian Democracy: A Formal Model of Regime Transitions." *Journal of Theoretical Politics* 25 (2).

Moore, M. 2004. "Revenues, State Formation, and the Quality of Governance in Developing Countries." *International Political Science Review* 25 (3): 297–319.

Moore, M. 2015. "Tax and the Governance Dividend." Working Paper 37, International Centre for Tax and Development, Brighton.

Murshed, M. S. 2009. "Conflict as the Absence of Contract." *The Economics of Peace and Security Journal* 4 (1): 32–38.

Ordor, A. 2020. "Human Rights as a Tool to Strengthen the Social Contract in Africa." Unpublished, World Bank.

Ozar, D. T. 1986. "Rights: What Are They and Where Do They Come From?" In *Philosophical Issues in Human Rights: Theories and Applications*, edited by P. H. Werhane, A. R. Gini, and D. T. Ozar. New York: Random House.

Paret, M. 2015. "Violence and Democracy in South Africa's Community Protests." *Review of African Political Economy* 42 (143): 107–23.

Phillips, S. G. 2020. *When There Was No Aid, War and Peace in Somaliland*. Ithaca, NY: Cornell University Press.

Piketty, T. 2018. "Brahmin Left vs Merchant Right: Rising Inequality and the Changing Structure of Political Conflict." Working Paper, Paris School of Economics. http:// piketty.pse.ens.fr/files/Piketty2018.pdf.

Prichard, W. 2015. *Taxation, Responsiveness and Accountability in Sub-Saharan Africa: The Dynamics of Tax Bargaining*. Cambridge, U.K.: Cambridge University Press.

Prichard, W., A. L. Custers, R. Dom, S. R. Davenport, and M. A. Roscitt. 2019. "Innovations in Tax Compliance: Conceptual Framework." Policy Research Working Paper 9032, World Bank Group, Washington, DC. http://documents.worldbank.org/curated /en/816431569957130111/Innovations-in-Tax-Compliance-Conceptual-Framework.

Rachman, G. 2019. "2019: The Year of Street Protest." *Financial Times*, December 23, 2019. https://www.ft.com/content/9f7e94c4-2563-11ea-9a4f-963f0ec7e134.

Resnick, D., and D. Casale. 2011. "The Political Participation of Africa's Youth: Turnout, Partisanship, and Protest." Working Paper 2011/56, UNU-WIDER, Helsinki.

Richards, P. 2020. "What Might Africa Teach the World? COVID-19 and Ebola Virus Disease Compared." *African Arguments*.

Riedl, R. B. 2014. *Authoritarian Origins of Democratic Party Systems in Africa*. London: Cambridge University Press.

Risse, T., and E. Stollenwerk. 2018. "Legitimacy in Areas of Limited Statehood." *Annual Review of Political Science* 21 (1): 403–18. https://doi.org/10.1146/annurev-polisci -041916-023610.

Ross, M. 2012. *The Oil Curse: How Oil Wealth Shapes the Development of Nations*. Princeton: Princeton University Press.

Rothstein, B., M. Samanni, and J. Teorell. 2012. "Explaining the Welfare State: Power Resources vs. the Quality of Government." *European Political Science Review* 4 (1): 1–28.

Sacks, A. 2012. "Can Donors and Non-State Actors Undermine Citizens' Legitimating Beliefs?" Policy Research Working Paper 6158, World Bank, Washington, DC. https:// doi.org/10.1596/1813-9450-6158.

Sebudubudu, D., and M. Z. Botlhomilwe. 2011. "The Critical Role of Leadership in Botswana's Development: What Lessons?" *Leadership* 8 (1): 29–45.

Soyemi, E. A. 2020. "COVID-19 and the Social Contract: A Lesson from Sub-Saharan Africa." *EUIdeas* (blog), May 8, 2020, European University Institute.

Stewart, F., ed. 2008. *Horizontal Inequalities and Conflict, Understanding Group Violence in Multiethnic Societies*. London: Palgrave Macmillan.

Tilly, C. 1990. *Coercion, Capital, and European States, AD 990–1990*. Oxford, U.K.: Blackwell.

Toska, S. 2017. "Sustaining Peace: Making Development Work for the Prevention of Violent Conflicts—Cases: Egypt, Tunisia, Morocco, and Jordan." Case study for the United Nations–World Bank Flagship Study, *Pathways for Peace: Inclusive Approaches to Preventing Violent Conflict*, World Bank, Washington, DC.

Transparency International. 2019. *Global Corruption Barometer: Africa 2019*. Berlin: Transparency International.

United Nations and World Bank. 2019. *Pathways for Peace: Inclusive Approaches to Preventing Violent Conflict*. Washington, DC: World Bank.

Usman, Z. 2020. "The Successes and Failures of Economic Reform in Nigeria's Post-Military Settlement." *African Affairs* 119 (474): 1–38.

Watts, M. 2019. "States, Societies and Citizenship: The Changing Social Contract in Post-Apartheid South Africa." Unpublished, World Bank, Washington, DC.

World Bank. 2004. *World Development Report 2004: Making Services Work for Poor People*. Washington, DC: World Bank.

World Bank. 2011. *World Development Report 2011: Conflict, Security, and Development*. Washington, DC: World Bank.

World Bank. 2012. "Global Partnership for Social Accountability and Establishment of a Multidonor Trust Fund." World Bank, Washington, DC. https://issuu.com/sholmberg /docs/gpsa_board_paper_june_13_2012.

World Bank. 2013. *Inclusion Matters: The Foundation for Shared Prosperity*. New Frontiers of Social Policy. Washington, DC: World Bank.

World Bank. 2017. *World Development Report 2017: Governance and the Law*, The World Bank: Washington, DC.

World Bank. 2018. *Engaging Citizens for Better Development Results*. Independent Evaluation Group, Washington, DC: World Bank.

Zeufack, A. G., C. Calderon, G. Kambou, C. Z. Djiofack, M. Kubota, V. Korman, and C. Cantu Canales. 2020. *Africa's Pulse*, No. 21 (April), World Bank, Washington, DC.

Zoellick, R. 2011. "The Middle East and North Africa: A New Social Contract for Development." Speech at the Peterson Institute, April 6, 2011.

Chapter 6

Development through a Social Contract Lens

Applying a social contract lens to development assistance, including to World Bank analytical and operational work, is important but also complex. The Independent Evaluation Group report (IEG 2019) concludes that a social contract framing can help diagnose complex development challenges such as entrenched inequalities, binding constraints, poor service delivery, weak institutions, and why decades of policy and institutional reforms promoted by external development actors have had uneven effects on countries' development paths. The report highlights the importance of this work given the growing use of social contract terminology in the World Bank's. However, the World Bank's lack of formal conceptual framework or shared understanding of social contracts, is leading to a wide variety of uses, sometimes not anchored in social contract theory or in a framework that can help trace a theory of change for reforms.

The focus of this report is to provide a conceptual framework to help client governments and World Bank staff in the application of a social contract lens to the development challenges faced in Africa. Chapter 2 of the report reviews the literature on social contract theory and its application and defines the concepts relevant to the regional context. Chapter 3 introduces a simplified empirical framework with which to measure important dimensions of social contracts in ways that can help provide an understanding of social contracts and the dynamics of change. In chapters 4 and 5 of the report, the concepts and framework are applied to country case studies and to specific sectors. These case studies and spotlights highlight the potential role of a social contract framing for country and sectoral diagnostics and policy design and implementation.

The conceptual framework and empirical operationalization, together with the more practical applications, can be a foundation for helping the region to develop standardized terminology and an adaptable empirical methodology that could facilitate the integration of a social contract lens into the World Bank's strategies, reports, and policy dialogue, as well as into the strategies and policy plans of governments and international organizations. The World Bank's country engagement tools—including Systematic Country Diagnostics, Country Partnership Frameworks, Risk and Resilience Assessments, and Recovery and Peace Building Assessments, among others—may be of interest.

For such country strategy documents, the analysis presented in this report can help leverage the benefits of a social contract framing. These benefits include (1) offering an integrated perspective connecting the different elements of a country's development spheres (political, social, and economic) in ways that help provide an understanding of what drives reforms and what makes them sustainable; (2) helping to anticipate indirect impacts of international aid on the social contract that could lead to unforeseen consequences, as well as the role of external shocks that can alter social contract dynamics and serve as opportunities for reform (or, on the opposite end of the spectrum, be a cause of, or at least provide justification for, rolling back progress); and (3) most important, placing citizens front and center of development efforts, not only as beneficiaries but also as major stakeholders with agency.

More work is needed to grasp the complexity of the social contract construct, and the remainder of this chapter explores unresolved questions and a potential path forward. First, a social contract diagnostics methodology could be developed to standardize the analysis for country or sector applications. To move forward with this effort, the empirical framework could benefit from multiple extensions, such as adding a time series dimension, adding subnational variations and considerations, and adding indicators to address the role of intermediaries and bargaining mechanisms. Second, the operational implications of a social contract lens need to be investigated more thoroughly. Third, the final section of the chapter discusses the considerations for whether and how the Bank can engage with social contracts, building on indications in IEG (2019) that the World Bank's engagement could be particularly useful in times of social contract transitions.

A Diagnostic: Understanding Social Contract Dynamics, Opportunities, and Obstacles to Reform

A next step in broadening the applicability of the social contract lens to policy design and implementation is to systematize social contract analysis at the country, subnational, or sectoral level (as appropriate). The diagnostic tool, a

Social Contract Diagnostic, would be based on a mixed-methods methodology that combines a quantitative analysis of a country's social contract aspects and dimensions with a qualitative analysis leveraging the knowledge of local scholars and stakeholders, along with the analysis of particular features of social contracts in Africa identified through this research program. As part of that methodology, the purpose of the framework would not be to impose assumptions on the nature of the social contract but to offer a lens through which to interpret the empirical data and a structure to guide the discussions with key stakeholders around mutually agreed-on concepts and definitions. The framework can therefore facilitate a more coherent and interactive dialogue between multidisciplinary contributions.

A Social Contract Diagnostic could involve the following main steps:

1. Identification of the research question and of any special topics to be addressed through a deep dive into some of the framework's dimensions or through an extension of the framework

2. Stock-taking of the literature and of the available data and identification of any data gaps and possible mitigation strategies, such as through rapid data collection methods (for example, targeted phone surveys, stakeholder mapping exercises, and so on)

3. Quantitative analysis of the empirical data based on the framework's structure, such as potential cross-country comparisons, subnational comparisons, and time series analysis

4. Identification of a broad list of local contributors to contact for interviews or more in-depth dialogue structured around the preliminary findings from the literature review and the empirical analysis; this step could also include focus group discussions, net-maps, individual interviews, academic workshops in which scholars are invited to present, a call for papers, and so on

5. Refining and qualifying the analysis of both the qualitative and quantitative data into a final report with realizable recommendations

As indicated, the quantitative indicators are at their most useful when they are combined with a qualitative approach to contextualize the measurements with local expertise. Together, the framework and qualitative approach form a mixed-methods assessment that could provide insights for illuminating chronic policy failure and identifying opportunities for reform, and how the Bank can engage with social contracts, as suggested by IEG (2019). This approach is being piloted through analytical work in Haiti and Somalia (box 6.1).

BOX 6.1

Application of the Social Contract Framing in Haiti and Somalia

Given the challenges of working with government at the central level in Haiti, an Advisory Services and Analytics effort was launched to look at the entry points for working at the subnational levels of government. A social contract framing was used to organize the analytical work. The rationale was that such a framing incorporates the double-sided nature of local governance: (1) an examination of the capability of public institutions necessary for service provision, including law and order, at the local level; and (2) an understanding of the degree to which citizens associate with authority and power. Such a framing is important in a context, such as Haiti, with weak state institutions for two reasons: first, to test sustainability and, over time, motivate citizens to pay taxes in return for service provision (Moore, Prichard, and Fjeldstad 2018); and second, to explore ways in which to strengthen basic trust in local authority, resulting in greater public safety and stability (McCullough 2020).

Building on this regional study, a World Bank team drafted the report "Understanding Somalia's Social Contract and State-Building Efforts: Consequences for Donor Interventions" (Cloutier et al., forthcoming). The paper investigates the country development challenges through the three social contract compasses of citizen-state bargaining, outcomes, and resilience. It uses the mixed qualitative and quantitative methodology to analyze the relative strengths and weaknesses of social contracts at different scales regarding security, taxation, and education.

Analysis to Understand Chronic Policy Failure and Identify Opportunities for Reform

The technical policy solutions being offered for chronic development challenges in Africa are relatively well known; the challenge is in their adoption and effective implementation. In this sense, a social contract lens is a means of applying the conceptual framework of the *World Development Report 2017: Governance and the Law* (World Bank 2017) to identify underlying constraints to policy effectiveness. IEG (2019, 15) concludes that "well-executed social contract diagnostics help teams understand policy failures, local political dynamics, and intractable development challenges and contribute to building partnerships." A number of Systematic Country Diagnostics in Africa[1] have referred to the need to strengthen the social contract as a means of reversing negative pathologies, but with an inconsistent, and often thin, analytical basis to explain what that really means and what is possible.

Adopting a deeper conceptual framing of the social contract as the outcome of bargaining dynamics that are shaped by a range of contextual factors can help keep the focus on a more concrete empirical analysis of relevant factors as outlined in this study's framework. Social contract analysis calls for an examination of the way societal groups bargain with the state to secure private or public goods, how a variety of factors shape the nature of the bargaining process and the bargains struck, and how these bargains enable or constrain progress on development outcomes. States shape citizenship and citizens shape states: it is this process of mutual constitution that stands at the center of robust social contracts. The Malawi Country Partnership Framework is grounded in this type of analysis (box 6.2).

BOX 6.2

Social Contracts in Malawi

"The social contract in Malawi has traditionally been described as revolving around the politics of maize. Since independence, the legitimacy of the government (and loyalty of the citizenry) has been linked closely with government promises to guarantee food. These vows have manifested through interventions in agriculture, starting with the creation of the marketing parastatal, the Agriculture Development and Marketing Corporation (ADMARC) in 1971 and continuing through targeted inputs, subsidies, and price stabilization interventions. While these extremely costly programs have served as tangible evidence of the government 'keeping its promise' to the people, they simultaneously keep citizens dependent on government food provision, crowd out other spending, and create opportunities for patronage via non-transparent pricing and procurement.

"The historic political change recently recognized in Malawi was spurred by mounting public frustration that the government was no longer holding up its side of the 'contract.' Public demonstrations around the disputed elections reflected deeper grievances against corruption, the lack of jobs, declining real wages, and poor-quality basic services. In the past, civil society groups and popular protest have limited attempts by the presidency to subvert democratic outcomes and constitutional limitations, but these movements faded away and were unable to change the underlying incentives facing incumbents. The question now is whether the momentum of collective action from the sustained, citizen-driven protests in 2019—in combination with increasingly mobilized urban youth, expanded access to information and technologies, and higher expectations of the new governing coalition—may begin to shift more sustainably the bargaining dynamics in the policy arena."

Source: Excerpt from World Bank 2021, 3.

This study does not provide all the answers but provides a framework as a starting point for developing a deeper understanding of citizen-state dynamics and situate World Bank engagement. In particular, the framework can be applied to gain a better understanding of sector reform in the following ways:

- This study puts forward a preliminary indicator framework, recognizing that it will need to be supplemented by additional investment in multidisciplinary use of nontraditional data sources, including barometer surveys, perception-based data, and political economy analysis. The study highlights the key elements of social contract bargaining that need to be understood: identification of the actors (state, nonstate, transnational) involved in the bargain, the power imbalances that shape bargaining dynamics, and key contextual factors that explain persistence or change opportunities.

- Although social contract analysis can help explain the "big picture" narrative and long-term trajectories, there is a rich complexity and variability within any given country at the level of specific development or sectoral challenges. More granular analysis of social contract bargaining around, for example, service delivery, social protection, security, business environment, political participation, and so on will help identify potential levers of change and programmatic implications, as well as potential trade-offs. Similarly, analysis of social contract dynamics at different spatial levels (for example, urban areas, lagging regions, or conflict-affected areas) will reveal asymmetrical possibilities for change.

How Can the World Bank and Other Partners Engage with Social Contracts?

On the one hand, it is overreaching to suggest that the World Bank can seek to shape social contracts in client countries, both as a matter of mandate and of ambition. On the other hand, by injecting resources, expert advice, and support into contested spaces, Bank interventions will inevitably have an impact on internal bargaining dynamics—by reinforcing the status quo, shifting relative power, or in some cases undercutting potentially positive bargaining dynamics. A social contract lens and theory of change regarding potential social contract impacts can be applied to World Bank programming as a *do no harm* principle at a minimum, and as a means of making informed choices.

Some operational considerations include the following:

- *Can the World Bank play a constructive role in renegotiation of the social contract?* Regime transition, postconflict state-building, or constitutional junctures may be important opportunities for the Bank to provide technical expertise, convening power, and credible signals of change on policy options with significant implications for social contracts, for example, around territorial and fiscal governance (federalism, decentralization, wealth sharing), addressing historical marginalization and inequalities, opening up economies, geographically targeted programming, and others.

- *Can the World Bank support opportunities at the national or subnational level to promote positive feedback loops between state capacity and citizen expectations?* Given asymmetric capabilities between state authority and citizens, opportunities may arise from realignment of conditions (for example, as emerged in the study on Lagos, Nigeria, around infrastructure and taxation). The challenge is to look beyond an individual reform champion to assess how the Bank can support a reform agenda, for example, in infrastructure, agriculture, or the private sector, to reinforce inclusive and responsive bargaining dynamics.

- *Can the World Bank use its citizen engagement mandate to strengthen bargaining mechanisms around particular policy areas (accountability, service delivery, business environment, and so on), both within and beyond individual projects?* A social contract lens requires looking beyond the narrow citizen engagement requirements that are specific to Bank projects to consider how interventions can have an impact on the underlying "rules of the game" in ways that reinforce positive bargaining dynamics around specific outcomes. This approach requires engaging with a broad set of stakeholders and building coalitions to enhance collective action capacity, strengthen the link between information transparency and state responsiveness, and foster multistakeholder platforms for policy dialogue. In this regard, the potential of disruptive technologies can also be explored (World Bank 2018).

- *Can the World Bank consider project design options incorporating a social contract lens that can help in identifying underlying distributional imbalances, the role of institutions, and citizen feedback loops?* For example, trade-off considerations can include the following:

  - Should infrastructure investments be partially reoriented toward those with strictly economic rather than broader-based gains?
  - How can the Bank balance a focus on the poorest of the poor with the need to support a growing middle class?
  - When implementing programs, should early emphasis be on pockets of effectiveness that can have positive demonstration effects or on lagging areas?
  - How should social programs be targeted in conflict-affected areas?
  - Do targeted interventions to support job creation entrench vested interests?

In short, the conceptual framework developed in this report, its application to the African context, and the illustrations on social contract thinking can be applied to better understand challenges and inform the design and implementation of sustainable reforms at the national and subnational levels. Systematically incorporating a social contract lens into the World Bank's development policy in the region and building on the insights from this report and the social contract work program can help make policy advice and support more sustainable, inclusive, and effective.

Note

1. For example, Malawi, Mali, Niger, Senegal, South Africa, Tunisia.

References

Cloutier, M., H. Hassan, D. H. Isser, and G. Raballand. Forthcoming. "Understanding Somalia's Social Contract and State-Building Efforts: Consequences for Donor Interventions." World Bank, Washington, DC.

IEG (Independent Evaluation Group). 2019. *Social Contracts and World Bank Country Engagements: Lessons from Emerging Practices*. Washington, DC: World Bank.

McCullough. 2020. "Reconstructing Our Understanding of the Link between Services and State Legitimacy." Working Paper 87, Secure Livelihoods Research Consortium, London.

Moore, M., W. Prichard, and O.-H. Fjeldstad. 2018. *Taxing Africa: Coercion, Reform and Development*. London: Zed Books.

World Bank. 2017. *World Development Report 2017: Governance and the Law*. Washington, DC: World Bank.

World Bank. 2018. *Engaging Citizens for Better Development Results*. Independent Evaluation Group, Washington, DC: World Bank.

World Bank. 2021. "Country Partnership Framework for the Republic of Malawi for the Period FY21–FY25." Report No. 154505-MW, World Bank, Washington, DC.